LINCOLN CHRISTIAN COLLEGE AND SEMINARY

HANDS-ON INFORMATION LITERACY ACTIVITIES

Jane Birks and Fiona Hunt

Neal-Schuman Publishers, Inc.

New York

London

Published by Neal-Schuman Publishers, Inc.
100 Varick Street
New York, NY 10013

Copyright © 2003 by Jane Birks and Fiona Hunt

All rights reserved. Reproduction of this book, in whole or in part,
without written permission of the publisher, is prohibited.
Printed and bound in the United States of America.

The paper used in this publication meets the minimum requirements of
American National Standard for Information Sciences—Permanence of Paper
for Printed Library Materials, ANSI Z39.48—1992. ∞

ISBN 1-55570-456-5

Table of Contents

105433

Foreword

Information literacy is a critical basic skill for the twenty-first century. As we venture into this new millennium, marked by the transition from an industrial to an information age, the invention and innovation fueled by modern science and technology have created a world of ubiquitous communication. Information surrounds and confounds us and will be the lifeblood of individual and collective progress in this century.

When I was young growing up in a small Texas town, our weekly trips to the local library were a highlight and I can still see the rows of shelved books and remember the sections I most loved to browse. Before I was 14 years old I had read most of the books in my favorite sections, so poor was our little local collection.

Today, that same library no doubt has electronic access to vast stores of information, and the friendly librarian no longer sits behind the checkout desk stamping books in and out and collecting overdue fines. Today, one does not even need a local library to access the information one needs. All it takes is a computer and basic information literacy skills. *Hands-On Information Literacy Activities* will help students hone those skills.

Jane Birks and Fiona Hunt have produced a practical and engaging book aimed at helping secondary school and college students develop critical information literacy skills. They are well qualified for this work, for they have developed and used many of these activities with students.

All of us today face this challenge. We can no longer depend on the enduring currency, relevance, or accuracy of our knowledge. We also can no longer depend on others to sift and sort information and package it for our convenient use. Using the tools provided by electronic communication, we can now access vast stores of information anywhere and anytime to serve the wide range of our information needs. But first, we must master the tools of making sense and effective use of it.

Hands-On Information Literacy Activities offers teachers and students hands-on experiences designed to develop information literacy skills. It focuses on key skills: the ability to determine the nature and extent of information needs, the ability to access information, and ways to critically evaluate information and its sources.

The learning activities presented in this book are interactive, and are designed to support a variety of learning styles by engaging students in actual information literacy process tasks. These learning activities have been tested and proved with secondary school and college students. They work!

B. Dell Felder, Ph.D.
Provost
Zayed University
U.A.E.

Preface

THE IMPORTANCE OF INFORMATION LITERACY INSTRUCTION

The rate of information production has increased exponentially, as has the capacity for storage of information, but our ability to read and comprehend has remained the same (Royce, 1999).

People need to be in control of information, they need to be able to harness it as required and use the relevant information as necessary. But they need more than just the information. They need to be information literate.

How do we teach information literacy skills effectively? What's the best way for our students to learn this critical ability? Research by Phillips (1984) validates the well-known axiom "we remember 10 percent of what we hear, 15 percent of what we see, 20 percent of what we hear and see, 60 percent of what we do, 80 percent of what we do with active reflection, and 90 percent of what we teach." While a great deal of information literacy instruction is presented as standard classroom lessons, *Hands-On Information Literacy Activities* embraces the concept of active learning with engaging, student-centered, activities.

We, the authors, are Information Literacy Librarians working at Zayed University, a women's university in the Arabian Gulf. Our students come to us with very little, if any, exposure to information literacy and the concepts of independent learning and critical thinking. Recognizing the growing need for practical materials in the field of information literacy instruction, we developed an interactive approach. Many of the activities we use have been adapted and used in a variety of situations with both ESL and native speakers of English.

Hands-On Information Literacy Activities contains practical ideas and all the necessary supporting instructional materials for teaching information literacy skills and concepts in an interesting, interactive manner. The activities are designed for teachers and librarians working with high school, community college, and undergraduate students. Teachers can use these activities independently, or in a team-teaching environment with another teacher or the librarian. How readers choose to present the activities will depend on the level of collaboration between instructors and librarians and the level of information literacy awareness.

Most of the lessons in *Hands-On Information Literacy Activities* have evolved from a librarian's perspective on accessing and evaluating information. We present them here in such a way that an instructor from any field would feel confident teaching the concepts. All activities have been tried and tested, initially by us as librarians and then by our collaborative teaching partners from various disciplines. We encourage you to use these materials and adapt them to meet both your own needs and the particular needs of your students.

HOW TO USE THIS BOOK

Hands-On Information Literacy Activities features twenty successful activities developed to help students master skills they will need to be information literate. Each activity is a fully contained event taking no longer than an hour. Supporting materials—handouts, worksheets, and answer keys—follow at the end of each activity. The supporting materials that follow the activities are sometimes abbreviated or reduced from their actual size, but all those mentioned in the text are included full size and in their entirety on the companion CD-ROM. When you click open the CD-ROM, you will find two files of support material, some of which are also found in the book. One file contains all sheets formatted in the horizontally arranged "portrait" layout; the other file contains all sheets formatted in the vertically arranged "landscape" layout. Because the material is separated this way, you will be able to print it all quickly in two batches without having to constantly change printer settings. Each file is sequentially ordered so that, if you are looking for an individual sheet, you need only check for the way that sheet appears in the book to determine if it can be found in the Portrait or the Landscape file on the CD-ROM. For the few items of support material that do not appear in the book, scroll through both files on the CD-ROM and you'll find you have a complete set. We invite you to use the CD-ROM material as is, or to customize it to suit your students' particular learning needs. Note that you will have to save the files onto your hard drive to alter them.

How you present the activities will depend largely on the level of the students, the time available for information literacy skill development, and the curriculum. The activities are presented sequentially as we have successfully introduced the concepts to our own students, building one segment on another. They can, however, be used in any order or any grouping.

ACTIVITY DESIGN

Each activity answers the following questions:

- What will the students learn?
- How much time will the instructor need?
- What materials or preparation are required?
- How does it work?
- Are there any pitfalls or pointers?
- What samples or support material can be used?

Please note that throughout the activities we employ parentheses to give non-verbal instruction or contain the expected or desired answer to questions the activity instructions direct you to ask the students. Also, all sample journal articles that appear in this book are fictitious and have been created to teach specific skills only.

The focus of the activities is on accessing information, something that students typically find difficult. The activities have been designed for maximum student participation and discovery. They are carefully structured to guide seemingly spontaneous classroom interaction towards the desired learning outcome.

Helping students develop their information literacy skills is a dynamic and engaging process. It is our sincere wish that the materials presented here will assist you in this process and contribute to your enjoyment and success in the information literacy classroom.

REFERENCES

Phillips, Gary. 1984. *Growing Hope*. Minneapolis, Minn.: National Youth Leadership Council.
Pritchett, P. 1993. *Culture Shift*. Dallas: Pritchett and Associates.
Royce, John. 1999. "Reading As a Basis for Using Information Technology Efficiently." In *The Information Literate School Community: Best Practice,* edited by J. Henri and K. Bonanno. Wagga Wagga, Australia: Center for Information Studies.

Acknowledgments

We would like to acknowledge the support provided to us by all of our colleagues in the library and in particular by those individuals who encouraged us when the enormity of trying to develop a program in a new university threatened to overcome us. Secondly, we owe a great deal to our original collaborative partners from the English department. Our partnership was forged through the recognition of a common desire for specific student outcomes and a willingness to exploit our various strengths in a joint venture. This particular joint venture has been extremely successful as a base on which our information literacy program is now being built, and it was as a part of this joint venture that the activities in this book were developed. Finally, we wish to thank all of the teachers with whom we have collaborated, who have given us invaluable feedback regarding the activities that follow.

Our Philosophy and How To Use This Book

INFORMATION LITERACY INSTRUCTION PHILOSOPHY

Today, information literacy instruction can take many forms, depending on the level of collaboration between teachers and librarians as well as the expertise and confidence of the different stakeholders in delivery of information literacy instruction. It can be a session taught in the library, by the librarian; it can be a session taught in a regular classroom with input from the librarian and/or the instructor; it can be taught in a session by the class teacher alone, using materials provided by the librarian. Information literacy sessions can be integral components of regularly scheduled courses or ad hoc sessions, planned and scheduled on an as-needed basis. It can also be independent, self-paced instruction using materials designed specifically for that purpose.

Active Learning

We believe strongly in the efficacy of instruction that supports active learning.

> This active engagement helps students integrate new material with what they already know. It helps them formulate new ideas in their own words and it helps students with a variety of learning styles understand the material in ways they would not if it was delivered in a lecture format. In short, it increases student's [sic] learning (Gradowski, Snavely, and Dempsey, 1998: vii).

Even so, the majority of instruction at the college or university level is delivered in lecture format, despite evidence in the literature that clearly indicates that alternative pedagogies are of great benefit to students (Siegfried et al., 1996).

Hands-On Information Literacy Activities embraces the concept of active learning.

MATRICES

We have written this section to provide you with an overview of the activities and make suggestions that you may find helpful when using these materials with your students.

Activities Grouped by Type, With Suggestions For Use

There are three types of activities in this book: games, assessment and review tools, and core activities. They are listed below under their appropriate headings, with our suggestions for their use.

Games

These activities can be introduced at any time, to review vocabulary or to reinforce concepts already learned. Use them at the beginning or end of a lesson, to start or finish on a high note, or in the middle to provide an energizing break for your students.

- Hot Seat/Concept Review Game
- What Are the Questions?
- Find Someone Who . . .

Assessment and Review

Like the games, these two activities can be introduced at any time. Before beginning a course of instruction, they can be used to assess students' prior knowledge of key information literacy concepts. After completion of study, they can be used to determine how much students have absorbed and identify areas for further development. Finally, it is often helpful to employ these tools both before and after the period of study to highlight for students the progress they have made and for students to identify for themselves areas in which they could develop further.

- **Information Literacy Preassessment** is a diagnostic tool to determine students' knowledge and abilities.
- **The Research Process** reviews the steps involved in carrying out research.

Core Activities

In this section, we present the remaining activities sequentially as we have successfully introduced the concepts to our own students, building one segment on another. By teaching these activities in the suggested order there is a natural progression of skill development. You will notice that we have grouped together, in boxes, interrelated activities that are best introduced together or closely following one another. The concepts explored by the activities in any one box are inextricably interwoven.

Of course, any reader can pick out isolated activities as they wish or need. Our recommendation—that some activities are best taught together rather than in isolation—is based on personal experience. For example, we have found that in order to understand databases fully and to search them effectively students first need to have a general concept of what a database is, then to understand how the computer searches a database. To do that properly they also need to understand and master Boolean logic and finally to apply the conceptual knowledge to a practical search situation using a "real" database available through their library.

The activities in the following boxes are interrelated in some way. In some cases, they follow on from each other and develop a concept or skill from a rudimentary to a more advanced level. In other cases, the activities deal with similar subject matter but don't necessarily need to be presented in the order shown below. For example, Search Engines could be introduced before or after Evaluating Web Sites I and II as it is on the same general subject (the Internet) but does not introduce or develop the concept. On the other hand, Evaluating Web Sites II should follow Evaluating Web Sites I as the second activity develops concepts introduced in the first. We have indicated these links and connections between activities later in the book, in the text of the instructions; the following layout is intended to give a visual overview for readers wishing to see how the activities fit together and interrelate.

Here, then, is the recommended presentation order of the activities. Each activity title is followed by a brief definition. Many activities cover a huge variety of material and we want to present a visual matrix to offer a clear idea of scope. For example, in Databases I and II, you can see that the first activity introduces the overall concept of a database and the next one provides practical, hands-on exploration of how a computer actually searches a database. We hope that this "at a glance" matrix will help when you are planning your information literacy sessions.

Library Orientation Treasure Hunt introduces students to the layout and services of the library.

Brainstorming Your Search Terms helps students organize their thinking.

Library Catalog explores the functions and features of the library catalog.

Search Engines examines the different kinds of search engines and how they search.

Evaluating Web Sites I identifies parts of a Web page and explores where to look for evaluation criteria.

Evaluating Web Sites II offers practice evaluating Web pages.

Databases I introduces the concept of a database.

Databases II investigates how a computer searches a database and demonstrates Boolean searching and truncation.

Boolean Frogs and Fish demonstrates Boolean logic using hands-on materials.

Boolean Attribute Shapes demonstrates Boolean logic using hands-on materials. This activity works better with a larger group.

Databases III explores the functions and features of a specific periodical database.

Search Strings provides practice formulating search strings.

Advanced Searching gives students practice anticipating search results, identifying potential problems, and troubleshooting.

Types of Information and Where To Find Them helps students identify the strengths and weaknesses of different sources, namely the Internet, periodical databases, and primary sources; it also helps students identify the best source for finding a particular kind of information.

Bibliography and Citation delves into the reasons you need to use a bibliography and explains the parts of a citation.

Note: Experience has shown that students must be aware of the need for a bibliography at an early stage in the research process so that they can keep track of their information as they search. However, instructors may choose to do a brief introduction earlier (for example, when they start searching) and cover the topic more thoroughly (by using this activity) at this stage.

Activities Grouped by Information Literacy Skill/Concept

The first matrix shows the activities grouped by type and in the suggested order of presentation. This second matrix offers a quick summary of what a student who masters the skills presented here will have accomplished. The goal of *Hands-On Information Literacy Activities* is to help instructors foster the development of information literate young people. Please note that our emphasis falls on accessing and evaluating information and most of the activities fall into those two categories. Students who master the skills and concepts introduced in this book will be well on their way to becoming fully information literate.

To be information literate, a person must be able to:

- determine the nature and extent of information needs
- access information

- evaluate information and its sources critically
- use information to communicate effectively to varied audiences in multiple contexts
- adhere to ethical practices in use of information

Activities that teach how to determine the nature and extent of information needs:
    Brainstorming Your Search Terms
    Search Strings
    Types of Information and Where To Find Them

Activities that teach how to access information:
    Library Orientation Treasure Hunt
    Library Catalog
    Search Engines
    Databases I
    Databases II
    Boolean Frogs and Fish
    Boolean Attribute Shapes
    Databases III
    Search Strings
    Advanced Searching
    Types of Information and Where To Find Them

Activities that teach how to evaluate information and its sources critically:
    Evaluating Web Sites I
    Evaluating Web Sites II
    Databases III
    Types of Information and Where To Find Them

Activity that teaches how to adhere to ethical practices in use of information:
    Bibliography and Citation

REFERENCES

Gradowski, G., L. Snavely, and P. Dempsey, eds. 1998. *Designs for Active Learning: A Sourcebook of Classroom Strategies for Information Education.* Chicago: Association of College and Research Libraries.

Siegfried, John J., Phillip Saunders, Ethan Stinar, and Hao Zhang. 1996. "Teaching Tools: How Is Introductory Economics Taught in America?" *Economic Enquiry* 43: 182–192.

ACTIVITIES

1

Hot Seat/Concept Review Game

Here's a fun way to review vocabulary and concepts already learned. Use it at the beginning of your class to review vocabulary and concepts for the lesson planned, midway through to energize your class and keep them focused, or at the end to finish on a positive high. We've provided a list of potential vocabulary, but feel free to adapt it as you wish.

WHAT WILL THE STUDENTS LEARN?

Students will demonstrate and review knowledge of information literacy vocabulary and concepts.

HOW MUCH TIME WILL I NEED?

You will need 15 to 20 minutes.

WHAT PREPARATION OR MATERIALS ARE REQUIRED?

- white board
- white board markers
- white board eraser
- two or three chairs
- list of vocabulary to use
- prizes (optional)

HOW DOES IT WORK?

1. Split the class into two or three teams.
2. Place a chair for each team at the front of the class, facing away from the white board and toward the students.
3. Invite one member from each team to come to the front and sit in their team's chair, known as the "hot seat."
4. Explain that you will write a word (or words) on the board. The person sitting at the front cannot see the word(s). Each team must define or describe that term (or concept) to their teammate in the hot seat. Their teammate must guess what the word is based on their definition or description.
5. Demonstrate once to make sure the students understand how it works.
6. Choose from your list of vocabulary and concepts, writing each one on the board in turn. The students will rotate into the hot seat after each person has guessed once or twice (depending on the size of the teams—ideally, you want everyone to have a chance in the hot seat).
7. Award one point to each correct answer. Half points can be awarded, as the instructor deems desirable, for ties, close answers, etc.
8. Optional: Award a prize to the winning team.

ARE THERE ANY PITFALLS OR POINTERS?

- This game starts slowly, but soon becomes fast-paced, so the instructor should have a long list of vocabulary at hand.
- It is best to keep the number of teams to two, as having more teams makes it difficult to keep track of correct guesses from the hot seats. Three teams is the maximum for the game to run smoothly.
- You will need to adapt the list of vocabulary in the support materials to fit the concepts and vocabulary appropriate for your own environment.

WHAT SAMPLES OR SUPPORT MATERIALS CAN I USE?

- Support Material 1: Sample List of Vocabulary and Concepts

SUPPORT MATERIAL 1:
SAMPLE LIST OF VOCABULARY AND CONCEPTS
FOR HOT SEAT/CONCEPT REVIEW GAME

Library catalog

Search string

Search strategy

Search term

Keyword

Information literacy

Citation

Bibliography

Boolean

Internet

Search engine

Web site

Bias

Evaluate

Research

Book

Journal

Encyclopedia

Periodical

Interview

Outline

Research proposal

Subject

Note taking

Plagiarism

Paraphrasing

Synthesizing

Brainstorming

Thesis statement

Argumentative thesis statement

Online/periodical databases

Library Web site

Newspapers

Newspaper files

Circulation desk

Reference desk

Reference collection

Electronic books

Library classroom

Almanac

Atlas

Dictionary

Primary sources

2

What Are the Questions?

Here's another enjoyable activity to use for vocabulary and concept review. As with Hot Seat, this game can be used at the beginning, middle, or end of a class to review vocabulary and concepts, energize students to keep them focused, or end on a high note.

WHAT WILL THE STUDENTS LEARN?

Students will demonstrate and review knowledge of information literacy vocabulary and concepts.

HOW MUCH TIME WILL I NEED?

You will need 15 to 20 minutes.

WHAT PREPARATION OR MATERIALS ARE REQUIRED?

- list of answers
- prizes (optional)
- buzzer/light (if possible, but not necessary); if not available, some other method of identifying the team that has responded first (noisemakers, and so forth—see *Are There Any Pitfalls or Pointers?* below)

HOW DOES IT WORK?

1. Divide the class into teams (two or three at most).
2. Explain that the game is designed to review vocabulary the students already know. The instructor will supply an answer and the students must think of the corresponding question and must phrase their response "What is . . . ?" The first team to hit the buzzer/put up a hand/reach the front of the classroom can guess at the question. (Devise the best method for your circumstances—see *Are There Any Pitfalls or Pointers?* below.) If they guess correctly, they will get a point. No point will be awarded for responses not beginning with the appropriate question word.
3. Give an example to ensure that they understand. For example: Answer: It is an animal with whiskers, pointed ears, and a long tail, and it likes to chase mice." Question: What is a cat?
4. Award a prize to the winning team after tallying the points (optional).

ARE THERE ANY PITFALLS OR POINTERS?

- It is essential to determine a fair way of identifying the team that will be allowed to guess the question. This game quickly gets out of control and it becomes difficult to determine who answered first. Here are some possible solutions:
  ◦ Use an electronic device with a light that allows only one response.
  ◦ Have a representative from each team run to the front of the class and take hold of an object, of which there is only one.
  ◦ Have two or three (however many teams there are) different types of noisemakers. You can tell which team responds first by the kind of noise they make.
- This activity works best if there are no more than three teams.

WHAT SAMPLES OR SUPPORT MATERIALS CAN I USE?

- Support Material 2: What Are the Questions? Worksheet
- Support Material 3: What Are the Questions? Answer key (see CD-ROM)

SUPPORT MATERIAL 2:
WHAT ARE THE QUESTIONS?

1. _____

   ANSWER: One is open and anyone can contribute information to it; the other is closed and only certain information is allowed in after an editor has looked at it.

2. _____

   ANSWER: It's used to find different variations of a word when you're searching.

3. _____

   ANSWER: Magazines, journals, and newspapers.

4. _____

   ANSWER: Library of Congress, or LC.

5. _____

   ANSWER: It tells you the subject of the book.

6. _____

   ANSWER: You can use it to find other books on the same subject on the shelves.

7. _____

   ANSWER: Authority or reliability, bias, usefulness, how current is it?

8. _____

   ANSWER: AND, OR, NOT.

9. _____

   ANSWER: Author, title, date, publication city, publisher, number of pages.

10. _____

    ANSWER: This allows people who read your paper to see where you got your information; it also protects you from being accused of plagiarism (stealing other people's ideas).

11. _____

    ANSWER: You use it to find books in the library.

3

Find Someone Who . . .

This is an activity that works well not only as a tool for reviewing vocabulary and concepts, but also for breaking the ice among students who may be unfamiliar with each other, as in the case of a new class or a class made up of individuals from different fields coming together for a one-time session in the library.

WHAT WILL THE STUDENTS LEARN?

Students will demonstrate and review knowledge of information literacy vocabulary and concepts.

HOW MUCH TIME WILL I NEED?

You will need 30 to 40 minutes.

WHAT PREPARATION OR MATERIALS ARE REQUIRED?

- Find Someone Who . . . worksheet
- white board
- white board markers
- white board eraser

HOW DOES IT WORK?

1. Explain that this activity is designed to review the students' knowledge of the vocabulary and concepts they have learned so far.
2. Write two examples on the board to demonstrate how the activity works:

Find Someone Who . . . .
. . . . Knows what a library catalog is
. . . . Knows what a search string is and can give an example

3. Pretend you are a student with a worksheet with these two questions on it. Ask one of the students, "Do you know what a library catalog is?" If they say "yes," write their name on the board next to that example. Ask another student, "Do you know what a search string is?" If they say "yes," write their name on the board next to the second example. If either student says "no," ask another student until you find someone who says "yes."

4. After doing these two examples, ask the first student to tell everyone what a library catalog is. Ask the second student to tell everyone what a search string is and give an example.

5. Check for comprehension:
   - What will you do? (Answer: Ask the other students the questions on the worksheet.)
   - Will you ask the same student all ten questions? (Answer: No.)
   - How many different names will you have on your sheet when you are finished? (Answer: Ten.)
   - Is it all right to say "yes" when you really don't know the answer? (Answer: No, because you will be asked to give the answer when the activity is over, in front of the whole class.)
   - Is it all right to give the worksheet to students and let them write their name next to an answer they know? (Answer: No, you must ask a student a question of your own choosing, orally!)

6. Give out the worksheets and monitor the students' activity. Make sure they are asking the questions and not just passing the worksheet around and getting people to write their name next to the ones they know. (This is important for ESL students, but perhaps less so for native speakers of English. With either group, however, it is more fun if the students ask each other the questions orally.)

7. When everyone is finished, go through the questions, asking for the name of a student who knows each piece of information. Ask that student for the answer. Ask the class if they agree or have anything to add to the answer. Work through all the answers in this way.

ARE THERE ANY PITFALLS OR POINTERS?

- This activity is teacher-led and requires a motivated class in order to work well.
- An alternate version is to give each student only one or two questions. Thus, each student will have a different set of questions. This way the students aren't repeating the same questions over and over again. To go over the answers at the end, use a master sheet with all the questions on it (the worksheet the students have in the version described above). Ask each question to the class and the student who has that question will supply the name of someone who knows the answer. That person will then tell the class what the answer is. This version has the potential to be more interesting, depending on the audience, because most of the questions will be unknown to the class as a whole.
- You may wish to adapt the Find Someone Who . . . Worksheet to include concepts and vocabulary specifically relevant to your students.

WHAT SAMPLES OR SUPPORT MATERIALS CAN I USE?

- Support Material 4: Find Someone Who . . . Worksheet
- Support Material 5: Find Someone Who . . . Answer key (see CD-ROM)

SUPPORT MATERIAL 4:
FIND SOMEONE WHO . . .

Who can name the librarians in the library?　＿＿＿＿＿＿＿＿＿＿＿＿

Who can list three rules of the library?　＿＿＿＿＿＿＿＿＿＿＿＿

Who knows what a library catalog is?　＿＿＿＿＿＿＿＿＿＿＿＿

Who knows what a Boolean operator is?　＿＿＿＿＿＿＿＿＿＿＿＿

Who knows how a database is different from
the Internet?　＿＿＿＿＿＿＿＿＿＿＿＿

Who knows what a bibliography is?　＿＿＿＿＿＿＿＿＿＿＿＿

Who knows why you should create a
bibliography?　＿＿＿＿＿＿＿＿＿＿＿＿

Who has successfully used a database to find
information?　＿＿＿＿＿＿＿＿＿＿＿＿

Who can list three things to look for
when evaluating a Web page?　＿＿＿＿＿＿＿＿＿＿＿＿

Who knows what a "search string" is?　＿＿＿＿＿＿＿＿＿＿＿＿

Who likes doing research?　＿＿＿＿＿＿＿＿＿＿＿＿

Who knows what "information literacy" means?　＿＿＿＿＿＿＿＿＿＿＿＿

4

Information Literacy Preassessment

Did you ever find yourself in an information literacy class where students complain, "We've done this before!" or "I already know how to use databases"? How much do your students bring with them where information literacy skill development and concept knowledge are concerned? This tool is helpful for determining students' entry level. Especially useful in classes where students are all at different levels, this tool will help you plan your classes in such a way that all students' needs can be met appropriately.

WHAT WILL I LEARN?

Instructors will be able to determine the student's prior knowledge to inform the planning of future instruction.

HOW MUCH TIME WILL I NEED?

You will need approximately 45 to 50 minutes.

WHAT PREPARATION OR MATERIALS ARE REQUIRED?

- Information Literacy Preassessment (student worksheet)

HOW DOES IT WORK?

1. Explain the purpose and hand out the worksheet to the students.
2. Allow the students to work through each question independently, or, if language level is an issue, they may work with the instructor. (Questions may be explained and clarified by the instructor, but if information literacy vocabulary or concepts are

not understood, questions should be left incomplete because this is the sort of feedback the instructor needs.)
3. Collect the completed worksheets for marking and collation of results.

ARE THERE ANY PITFALLS OR POINTERS?

*   This is a diagnostic tool that may be used to inform the teaching/learning process.
*   There are many acceptable answers for these questions and in most cases there is no definitive "correct answer."

WHAT SAMPLES OR SUPPORT MATERIALS CAN I USE?

*   Support Material 6: Information Literacy Preassessment (student worksheet; see CD-ROM)
*   Support Material 7: Information Literacy Preassessment (answer key; see CD-ROM)

5

The Research Process

Imagine you have a group of students who have presumably been writing papers in one form or another since early high school days, perhaps even elementary school, yet when you ask them to write a research paper, there are still blank faces and many students have no idea where to start. This activity includes a puzzle that will help students identify and review the steps they go through to do research and write a paper.

WHAT WILL THE STUDENTS LEARN?

- Students will identify the main steps required to carry out research for a written paper or oral presentation.
- Students will recognize the cyclic nature of the research process, realize that many steps need to be done again and again, and understand that individuals may carry out the steps in a different order.

HOW MUCH TIME WILL I NEED?

You will need approximately 30 minutes.

WHAT PREPARATION OR MATERIALS ARE REQUIRED?

- The Research Process—laminated puzzle sets
- The Research Process—laminated answer keys (not cut up)
- white board
- white board markers
- white board eraser
- oversize flip chart
- markers for students to use on flip charts

HOW DOES IT WORK?

1. Ask the students to think about how they would teach a friend to go about doing research.
   a) What steps should they follow?
   b) What would you tell your friend?
   c) How should they start? For example, what would you tell them to do first? (Possible answers: Get a topic, work out what information they need by brainstorming possible content and approaches.)

2. Spend a few minutes brainstorming the main points or steps needed for research by either
   a) eliciting responses from the group and listing on the board, or
   b) dividing students into groups of three or four. (Provide pen and paper for each group. Have them write their ideas on a piece of paper, preferably a large flip chart so the whole class can see what is written.)

3. Call the groups together after a few minutes and elicit the main points. List these on the board, or have the students hold up their flip chart paper and compare.

4. Write the main steps from Support Material 8 (page 28) on the board and discuss the relationship between these and the students' suggestions. Hopefully there will be some correlation.

5. Tell the students that you (the instructor) have identified one way of proceeding through the research process (there are others) and, if we take these as the main steps, you want them to think about and discuss what each of the substeps would be.

6. Hand out the packs of puzzle pieces and ask each group to:
   a) Start with the puzzle piece The Research Process and place it at the top of their work space.

b)   Pick out the main steps (point out that these are the longer pieces of the puzzle and should match the steps written on the board in step 3) and lay these out in sequence one under another leaving plenty of space between each one.

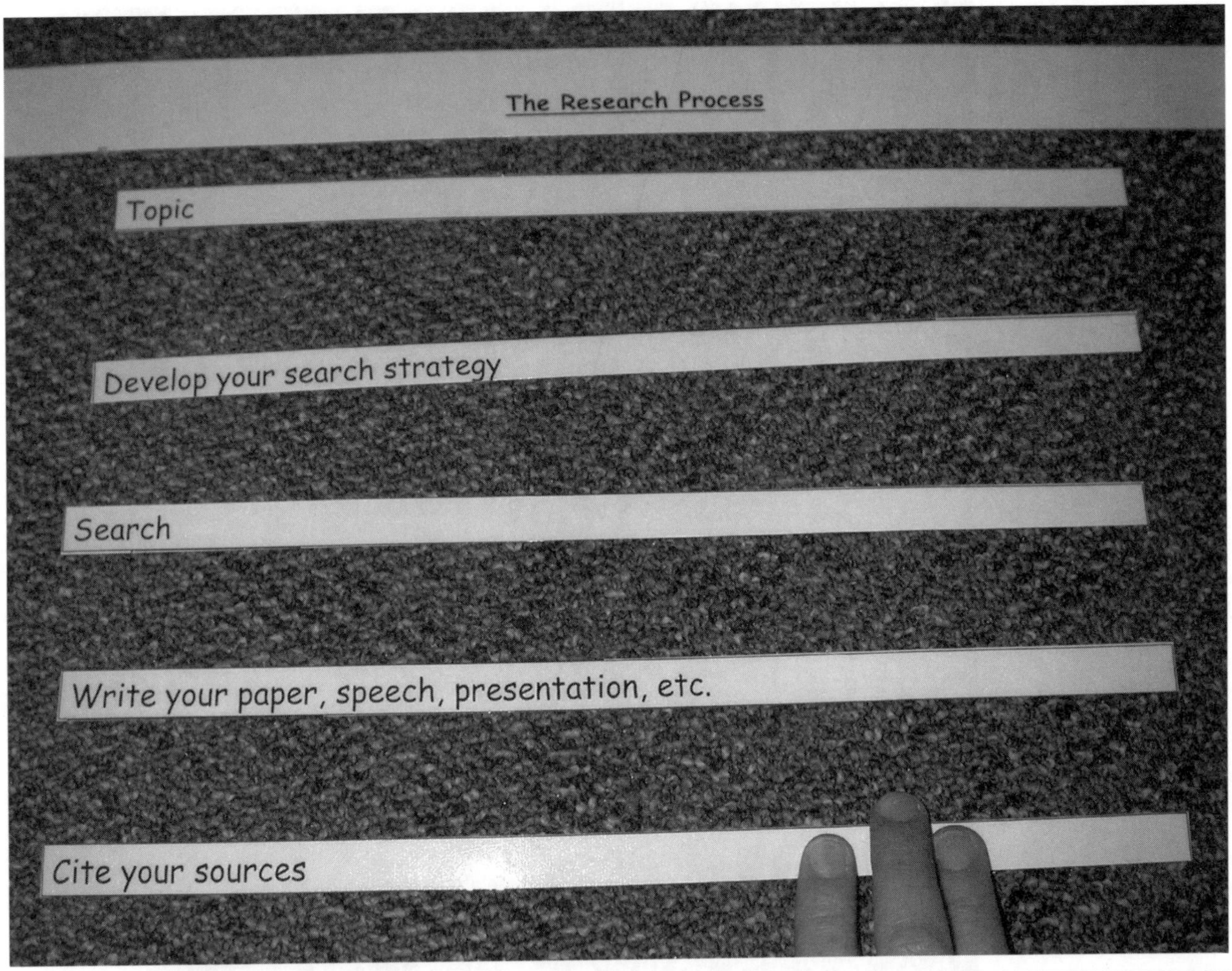

The Research Process

Topic

Develop your search strategy

Search

Write your paper, speech, presentation, etc.

Cite your sources

Figure 5–1. Students should start with the heading "The Research Process" and place it at the top. Next, they should pick out the main steps (point out that these are the longer pieces of the puzzle and should match the steps written on the board in step 3) and lay these out one under another leaving plenty of space in between each one.

c) Sort each of the substeps and lay them out under each main step to show the order you think most suitable.

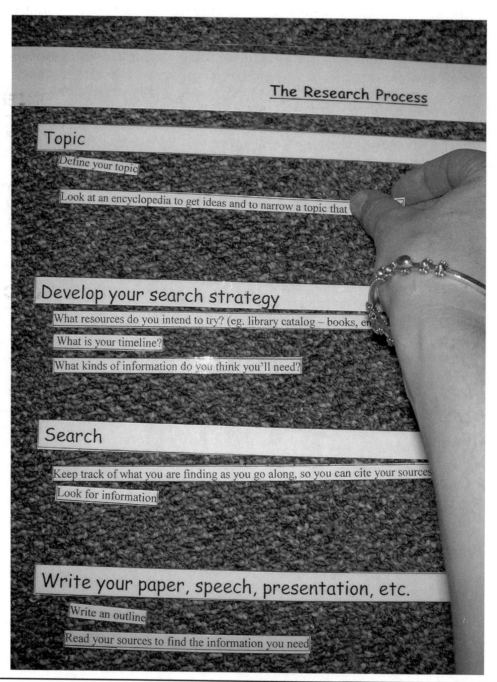

Figure 5–2. The thinner strips with the details of the steps involved in the research process should then be placed underneath the appropriate main headings.

7. Walk around to each group as they work and discuss why they are making the choices that they are.
8. Provide each group with the key as they finish. Ask them to compare their group's order with the order on the key but not to change their order.
9. Discuss both a) the nature of any differences and b) the reasons why various groups had different orders.

ARE THERE ANY PITFALLS OR POINTERS?

- This puzzle is one possible example. You may feel strongly about the sequence or wording and may want to create your own example showing different steps in a different order.
- It is essential for students to realize that there are many ways to approach the research process; although various components must be present, they may be done in a variety of different sequences and many steps need to be repeated as students proceed through the process.

WHAT SAMPLES OR SUPPORT MATERIALS CAN I USE?

- Support Material 8: The Research Process
  - To make the puzzle sets of The Research Process, copy the support material onto different colors in A3/11"x17" size paper and laminate and cut them to create your own set of puzzle pieces.
  - Each group should have a different colored set to avoid puzzle pieces getting mixed up. We have found that three students to a group works well.
  - Use Support Material 8 again, copying to A4/8$\frac{1}{2}$x11-inch paper as an answer key. We suggest you copy this in the same colors so each key will match one of the puzzle sets.

SUPPORT MATERIAL 8:
THE RESEARCH PROCESS

GET A TOPIC

Define your topic

Look at an encyclopedia to get ideas and to narrow a topic that is too broad

Think about specifics to narrow a topic that is too broad

Think about what kinds of information you'll need

Think about where you'll find your information

Think about your timeline

Brainstorm search terms—narrower, broader, synonyms—to make you more flexible while searching

DEVELOP YOUR SEARCH STRATEGY

Think about your timeline

Write an outline

Think about resources you intend to try (for example, library catalog, books, encyclopedias, journals, the Internet, WWW, databases, interview)

Think about which search terms/string(s) you will use

SEARCH AND READ

Look for information

Evaluate the information you find—is it relevant and is it reliable?

Redefine your topic and search terms as you go, depending on what you find

Keep track of what you are finding as you go along, so you can cite your sources accurately later

Read your sources

Take notes

Include a good variety of sources and up-to-date information whenever appropriate

Keep searching or stop, depending on what you've found

WRITE YOUR PAPER, SPEECH, PRESENTATION, AND SO FORTH

Rewrite an outline if necessary

Read your notes to find the information you need

Rewrite from your notes, in your own words

Go back to your sources and take more notes if necessary

Read through your paper—checking content and language

CITE YOUR SOURCES

Write a bibliography

6

Library Orientation Treasure Hunt

Another aspect of the transition from high school to university that many students find daunting is the actual physical space that confronts them when they venture into the library. This activity is fun and will help students feel at home and confident about using the facility. The exercise is designed to send the students off on a race of discovery around the library.

WHAT WILL THE STUDENTS LEARN?

Students will understand the library's layout and learn about its resources, services, and staff.

HOW MUCH TIME WILL I NEED?

You will need 20 to 30 minutes.

WHAT PREPARATION OR MATERIALS ARE REQUIRED?

- A map of your library.
- Library Orientation Treasure Hunt worksheet. You may wish to use our questions (Support Material 9) as a guide, but redesign the Treasure Hunt to suit your own physical space and services. We have designed it with the specifics of our library in mind.
- Prizes. These are optional, but we like to add to the fun of this activity by telling our students that there will be a "fabulous" prize for the team that wins. We then start some speculation as to whether it will be a sports car or perhaps a diamond bracelet. When we finally announce the winning team, we explain that the prize is in fact a irresistible luxury item as we bring out pocket-size chocolate bars.

HOW DOES IT WORK?

1. Give the students a map of the library and a Library Orientation Treasure Hunt worksheet.
2. Divide the students into pairs or small groups. We find that three is the maximum size for a group.
3. Inform the students that they have a limited time (say, 15 to 20 minutes) to find answers to the questions, with the map as their reference.
4. Explain to the students that the team or pair that finishes first will receive a "fabulous" prize (optional).
5. Reassemble the students after the allotted time is up.
6. Discuss the answers that the students came up with to ensure they now understand the layout of the library and what services are offered.
7. Ask them to list three of the library's rules (optional).

ARE THERE ANY PITFALLS OR POINTERS?

- The map and treasure hunt worksheet are examples only and will need to be redesigned for your site.
- Be aware that if students are in groups that are too large some students may not benefit from the activity because they may rely on the others to find the information.
- When discussing the answers, use any questions that arise as impromptu teaching points to guide the discussion.
- Library staff need to be briefed ahead of time that they may be approached for answers to these questions. They can give hints, but should try to avoid direct answers. Hints could include directing students to read signs, suggesting they look at titles on the shelves, or asking a leading question to get them thinking along the right track.

WHAT SAMPLES OR SUPPORT MATERIALS CAN I USE?

- Support Material 9: Library Orientation Treasure Hunt Sample Worksheet
- Support Material 10: Map of Library (sample only)
  - This map will need to be copied and laminated for each group. The map should be marked with letters indicating the location of facilities the students will be asked to identify. For example, the reference desk could be marked with an *A* so the students can be quizzed as to what purpose the facilities at spot *A* serve. We keep a collection of these maps in the library so any group that comes through can use and reuse them.

SUPPORT MATERIAL 9:
LIBRARY ORIENTATION TREASURE HUNT

1. Look at your library map. What is the correct name for the area or facility marked **A**? What do you do there?

   _____

2. Where is the room where library classes are taught?

   _____

3. a) Where is the general collection? b) What do you find there? c) What subjects are these resources about?

   _____

4. Where is the best place to go for information on our country? What is the name of this collection?

   _____

5. Where can you plug in your laptop to use it in the library?

   _____

6. Where is the Reference Desk? What can you do there?

   _____

7. Where can you find the videos?

   _____

8. Where can you find a magazine?

   _____

9. Where are the newspapers kept? a) current _____

   b) older issues _____ c) newspaper files_____

10. Where can you find the Head Librarian?

   _____

11. Where can you find the library catalog? What would you use it for?

   _____

SUPPORT MATERIAL 10:
MAP OF LIBRARY (SAMPLE ONLY)

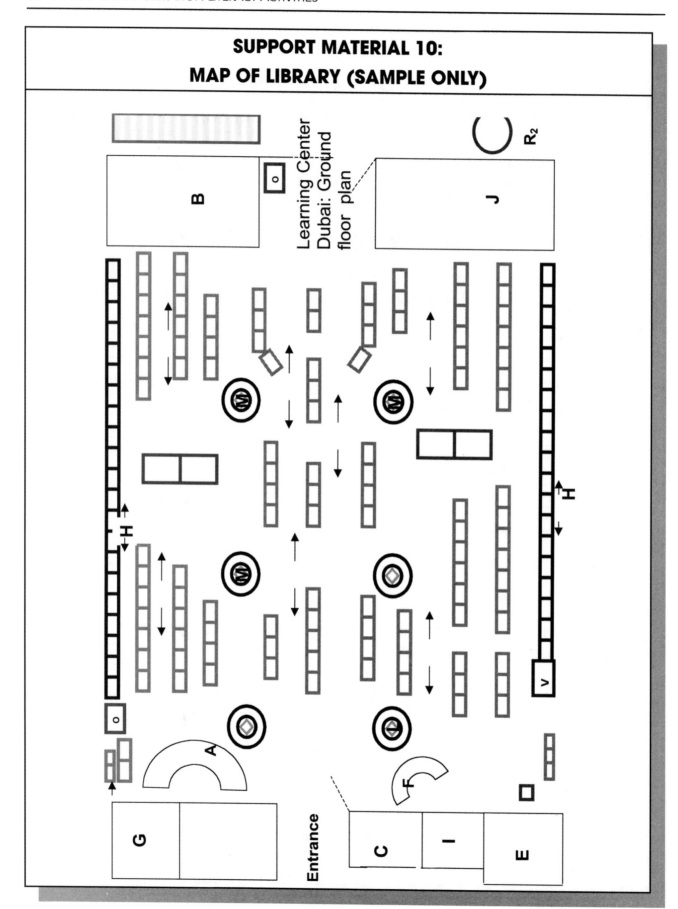

Learning Center
Dubai: Ground
floor plan

Entrance

7

Brainstorming Your Search Terms

Now that the students are familiar with the physical surroundings of the library and the resources available to them, it is time to begin the research process. Whether they choose their own research topic or thesis statement or whether they have one assigned will depend on the research activity itself.

This should be a quick exercise that students will benefit from repeating each time they begin a research project. Not only will it help them with their searching by supplying relevant search terms, it will also help them explore all aspects of their topic.

WHAT WILL THE STUDENTS LEARN?

Students will gain practice identifying the main ideas (keywords) in their research question and brainstorming for synonyms and broader, narrower, and related terms in preparation for beginning their search.

HOW MUCH TIME WILL I NEED?

You will need 30 to 50 minutes, depending on the class.

WHAT PREPARATION OR MATERIALS ARE REQUIRED?

- Brainstorming Your Search Terms worksheet
- white board
- white board markers
- computer and LCD projector

HOW DOES IT WORK?

1. Write a sample research question at the top of the white board. For example: Does television promote aggression in children? (Another good example is How does pollution affect birds in __ (country) __?)
2. Ask the class to identify the main ideas. (Answers: Television, children, aggression.)
3. Write **main idea #1**, **main idea #2**, and **main idea #3** inside three giant bubbles (you could use circles if you prefer) across the board (see Figure 7–1) with the research question at the top of the board. Explain that these main ideas are called keywords and write each keyword identified by the class in the middle of one of the giant bubbles.

Figure 7–1. Brainstorming your Search Terms – shows how the keywords are written on the whiteboard, in the bubbles – one bubble per keyword.

4. Explain that we will now brainstorm for words related to each keyword. Start with *television* and use it as an example for the whole class to do together.
5. Begin by asking for synonyms (for example, TV). Write any synonyms the class supplies in the bubble with the keyword *television* (for example, television=TV).
6. Ask now for more specific terms: What kinds of things do you see on TV? What kinds of things could belong to the category *television*? (Answers: Cartoons, advertisements, movies, music videos, and so forth.) Write these terms in the bubble underneath the keyword *television*.

7. Ask for broader terms: *Television* belongs to what bigger idea/concept/category? (Answers: Media, entertainment industry, communications industry, and so forth.) Write these terms in the bubble above the keyword *television*.
8. Now ask for related terms: What ideas are related to *television*? (Answers: Broadcasting, magazines, popular culture, and so forth.) Write these terms in the bubble to the left of the keyword *television*.

Figure 7–2. Related terms are filled in to make one complete bubble.

9. Explain that you would like the students to do this same exercise for the remaining two keywords.
10. Give out the worksheet Brainstorming Your Search Terms (Support Material 11).
11. Conduct a quick check to make sure everyone knows what to do.
12. Give the students time to complete the exercise. You may need to help them substantially with their brainstorming. Their adeptness with this activity will depend greatly on their mastery of English vocabulary and their familiarity with the concepts of classification and categorization.
13. Gain the class's attention when most of the students have completed the exercise and have identified a number of synonyms and narrower, broader, and related terms. Elicit their brainstorming ideas and write them onto the white board.

14. Redefine as necessary the terms suggested by the students or point out that some do not fit. Again, their success with this exercise will depend on their past experience and mastery of English.

15. Ask the class, "Why have we done this? Why would this be useful for searching?" (Their answers will depend once again on their past experience. You can lead them to the correct answer, as outlined below.)

16. Ask the students what happens when they do a search. Do they find everything they need the first time? (Answer: Not always.) What do they do when they don't find what they need? (Answer: Change search terms.)

17. Demonstrate how the brainstorming exercise will help them when they face a search that doesn't go anywhere or that doesn't find enough information. Read the research question several times, substituting words from the class's brainstorming. For example:

   a) Do **cartoons** promote aggression in children?
   b) Do **movies** promote aggression in children?
   c) Does television promote **violence** in children?
   d) Does television promote aggression in **preschoolers**?

   After reading each substitution, ask the class if information that might be found using the substituted word would still be useful for their research project? (The answer should be yes.)

18. Do a search to demonstrate this idea in real life. Open the library catalog and project it onto the screen or white board.

19. Do a search for a topic that will not bring up many hits. (An example we use is *elephants* since ours is a small collection. You may need to use a more obscure term to ensure that the number of hits is low in your own library.) Ask the students what else we could try to get more hits. (Our students usually suggest *animals*, *wildlife*, and, with prompting, *Africa* and *India*.) Point out that within a book on a broader subject there may well be information about our more specific topic; we can find it using the index or table of contents of the book.

20. Finally, ask the class how they will come up with synonyms and narrower, broader, and related terms if the topic is a new one for them and one with which they are unfamiliar. (Answers: Read an encyclopedia article to get a sense of the topic and to find potential keywords; use a thesaurus; use a dictionary; and, once they have begun searching, look for related keywords that appear in the information they find.)

21. Explain that this is an exercise they would benefit from repeating each time they begin a research project. Not only will it help them with their searching by supplying relevant search terms, it will also help them explore all aspects of their topic.

ARE THERE ANY PITFALLS OR POINTERS?

- As suggested above, this activity may go very quickly or very slowly, depending on the class. First-language speakers of English and students from an educational tradition that emphasizes critical thinking should have fewer problems coming up with the necessary vocabulary and should be familiar with the concepts of classification and categorization. Students speaking English as a second or foreign language will likely have more trouble with the vocabulary, and students from educational traditions that emphasize memorization and rote learning may have difficulty with the concept of classification.

- This activity is best used at the beginning of the research process, as the students are beginning to think about their topics and before they have begun searching for information.

WHAT SAMPLES OR SUPPORT MATERIAL CAN I USE?

- Support Material 11: Brainstorming Your Search Terms Worksheet

SUPPORT MATERIAL 11:
BRAINSTORMING YOUR SEARCH TERMS

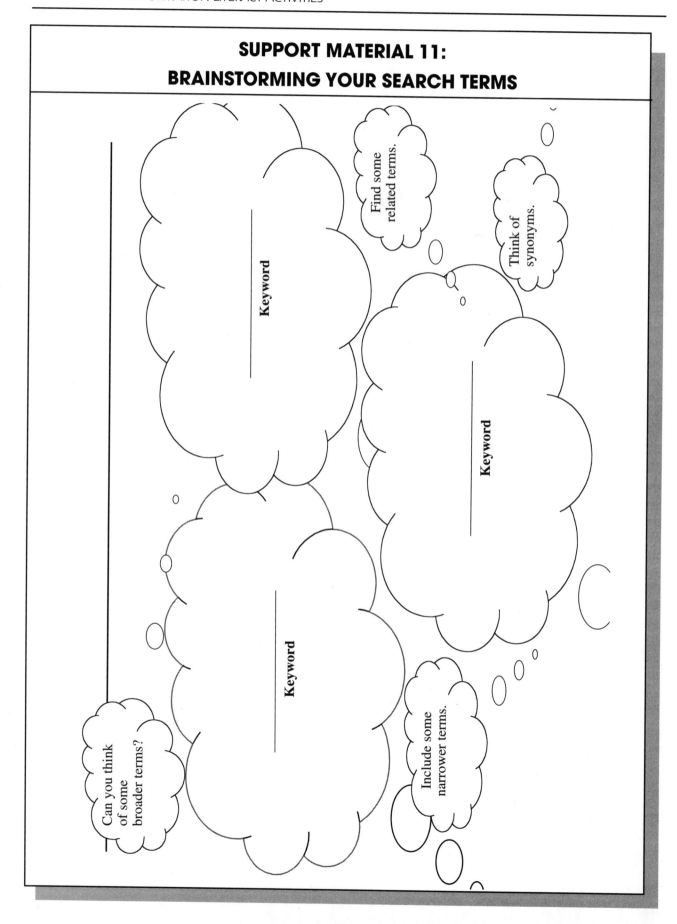

Keyword

Keyword

Keyword

Find some related terms.

Think of synonyms.

Can you think of some broader terms?

Include some narrower terms.

8

Library Catalog

The next step is to begin the search for potential information sources. Regardless of whether students have previously used an online catalog or not, they will all benefit from an exercise that guides them through the search process in your institution, highlighting the unique features of your library catalog.

WHAT WILL THE STUDENTS LEARN?

Students will learn how to use the library catalog and apply proper search techniques.

HOW MUCH TIME WILL I NEED?

You will need 40 to 60 minutes.

WHAT PREPARATION OR MATERIALS ARE REQUIRED?

- Library Catalog Worksheet (adapted to your institution's system)
- computer for instructor and each group of students
- LCD projector for instructor
- screen or white board to project onto

HOW DOES IT WORK?

1. Hand out worksheet and ask the students to work through it, following the directions and answering the questions.
2. Stop them at various points throughout the worksheet to explain or clarify details if necessary. (These details may have to do with the catalog itself, or more generally, with search technique or searching concepts.)
3. Have an answer key ready, either for going over the answers later with the students or for students to check their own answers. If you have been stopping the students

throughout the exercise to explain details, most problematic areas will already have been dealt with and the answer key should not provide the students with many surprises.

ARE THERE ANY PITFALLS OR POINTERS?

- See the sample provided in the *What Samples or Support Materials Can I Use?* section (below). Each institution will have its own library catalog and a unique student population; this material will likely need to be adapted for your particular circumstances.
- The sample that is included on the CD-ROM was designed with the following aims in mind:
  - to explain the features of the online catalog
  - to allow the students to discover these features by doing, not by reading explanations of them
  - to teach and review search techniques and concepts such as truncation, keyword versus field searching, narrowing or broadening a search, and so forth
  - to emphasize wherever possible training the students to read the search screen and rely on themselves to figure out how the various functions of the catalog work.

WHAT SAMPLES OR SUPPORT MATERIALS CAN I USE?

- Support Material 12: Library Catalog Worksheet (sample only; see CD-ROM)

9

Search Engines

Continuing the search for information, students may now wish to turn to the Internet. This hands-on activity will make your students better information seekers. Although most students have a favorite search engine, Yahoo! and Google being two notable examples, few understand the limitations of these engines or that there are different types of search engines available to them that search in different ways.

The most appropriate time to use this activity has been hotly debated in our program. We consider this a more advanced activity. However, since most students are familiar with the Internet and are comfortable using it, we feel that it should be introduced earlier rather than later, but it may require some preteaching of the concepts of Boolean operators, truncation, and so forth. You may also choose to use this activity after Databases I (page 77), II (page 89), and III (page 107), when students will have a better understanding of these concepts.

WHAT WILL THE STUDENTS LEARN?

Students will

- understand that there are different types of search engines
- explore the benefits and drawbacks inherent in each type
- examine several search engines and become familiar with their main features

HOW MUCH TIME WILL I NEED?

You will need 60 minutes.

WHAT PREPARATION OR MATERIALS ARE REQUIRED?

- computer
- LCD projector
- white board
- Blu-Tak or similar adhesive putty

- Search Engines Worksheet—Instructor's Guide
- Search Engines Worksheet—Student Handout
- Card Set—Types of Search Engines
- Card Set—Definition of Each Type of Search Engine
- Card Set—Benefits and Drawbacks of Search Engines (some of these cards are duplicated, as they apply to more than one category)
- blank chart for students to fill in, with one example provided
- *www.google.com*
- *www.yahoo.com*
- *www.metacrawler.com*

HOW DOES IT WORK?

1. Begin by asking the students what the different kinds of search engines are. They may or may not know and will probably not know them all.
2. Explain that this lesson will look at the different types of search engines on the Internet and how they search.
3. Begin by putting the cards **Subject Guide/Directory**, **"Live" Search Engine**, and **Meta Search Engine** (Support Material 15) up on the board. Place them along the top of the white board with space underneath each one for further cards.
4. Tell the class these are the three main types of search engines. Ask the students for their ideas about what each type does. They may be stumped, but this will give them an opportunity to puzzle it over and be interested in finding the answer.
5. Tell them you're going to show them examples of all three types, one at a time, not in the above order. They must try to figure out which is which.
6. Project onto the screen or white board *www.yahoo.com*.
7. Do a search by clicking on one of the subject categories under the search box. Then click on one of the subcategories that appears. Point out that with each click, we are going further into the subject and getting more and more specific. We are following a path through categories and subcategories. Follow one search path to its end to demonstrate how far you can go into a subject.
8. Type a term into the search box in Yahoo!. In the results list, show the class where it says, beside each result, which subject path the search engine followed to find that result. Ask them what that means. (Answer: It means that the search engine searched within the subject categories we just explored—essentially, the search engine is not searching "live" but is looking in sites that have already been chosen and categorized by Yahoo!.)
9. Ask the class if they know which type of search engine Yahoo! is. (Answer: Subject guide or directory.) If they don't know, move on to the next search engine anyway.
10. Project *www.google.com* onto the board or screen.
11. Do a search by clicking in the search box.
12. Look at the results. What do the students see? Does it look the same as the results in Yahoo!? What are the differences? (Google is both a "live" search engine and a subject guide or directory. Direct students' attention toward the two types of results that you get when you do a search: a) those with the categories listed, as with Yahoo!, and b) those without categories, "live" results.)

13. Ask the students to guess which kind of search engine Google is.
14. Move on to the next search engine, regardless of whether they guessed correctly or not. Ask them to keep observing and to remember what we discovered with each example.
15. Project *www.metacrawler.com* onto the board or screen.
16. Do a search. Examine the results together as above. How is Metacrawler different from the other two search engines? (Answer: The main difference is that Metacrawler shows which search engines it used to find each result; there will probably be at least two search engines listed with each result, but not always.)
17. Ask the students if they can identify which type of search engine each example is after showing all three kinds.
18. Give out the cards with the definitions on them. This can be done in three different ways, as you wish:
    a) You can give them out by dividing the class into three groups and giving each group one definition card. Depending on the size of your class, the groups could be quite large.
    b) You may wish to copy the card set several times and divide the class into groups of two or three; each group will get a complete card set (that is, eight cards).
    c) You could choose to put the definition cards on the white board, perhaps down the side of the board so they do not fall under any of the search engine type cards along the top of the board.

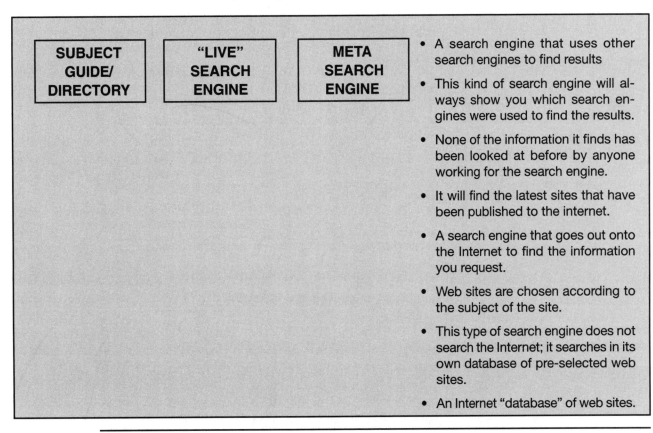

Figure 9–1. Types of search engines and definitions are shown down side of board.

Whichever way you choose, the students will put their cards, or tell you where to put them (if you choose option *c*), underneath the correct search engine type on the white board.

SUBJECT GUIDE/ DIRECTORY	"LIVE" SEARCH ENGINE	META SEARCH ENGINE
• An Internet "database" of web sites. • This type of search engine does not search the Internet; it searches in its own database of pre-selected web sites. • Web sites are chosen according to the subject of the site.	• A search engine that goes out onto the Internet to find the information you request. • It will find the latest sites that have been published to the internet. • None of the information it finds has been looked at before by anyone working for the search engine.	• A search engine that uses other search engines to find results • This kind of search engine will always show you which search engines were used to find the results.

Figure 9–2. Definitions are under correct headings.

19. Discuss with them which example (Yahoo!, Google, Metacrawler) is described by each card (if they didn't already guess correctly above).
20. Go back over each example from above (Yahoo!, Google, Metacrawler), referring to the appropriate definition on the board, pointing out why it qualifies as that type of search engine. Try to elicit this information from the students whenever possible.
21. Ensure that they understand the differences between the types of search engines and the different ways they search, then ask the class for their ideas about the benefits and drawbacks of using each type.
22. Brainstorm and write these ideas on the white board under the appropriate search engine card.
23. Give out the cards that describe the benefits and drawbacks, one card for each two or three students. This can be done in three different ways, as you wish:
    a) You can give them out by dividing the class into three groups and giving each group a number of cards. Depending on the size of your class, the groups could be quite large.
    b) You may wish to copy the card set several times and divide the class into groups of two or three; each group will get a complete card set (for example, 12 cards—remember to duplicate some of these according to Support Material 18).
    c) You could choose to put the drawbacks and benefits cards on the white board, perhaps down the side of the board so that they do not fall under any of the search engine type cards along the top of the board.

24. Let the students complete the task of placing the benefits and drawbacks cards under the appropriate headings on the board.
25. Discuss the results. See Support Material 18 for the answer key.
26. Ask the class what kinds of information would be best found with each type of search engine. For instance, "live" search engines are good for breaking news and the most up-to-date information. A subject guide/directory is good for finding relevant information and an overview of a subject. Metasearch engines are excellent at finding superficial information that may give ideas for keywords and more in-depth searching.
27. Show the students the chart (Support Material 19) with the different features of the search engine filled in for the example in the first column. Discuss and clarify the search concepts listed down the left-hand side of the chart. Students may have been introduced to these concepts previously. If not, a preteaching session may be necessary before this activity is presented. Once you are sure they understand these concepts, ask the students where to find this type of information for a particular search engine (Answer: The information should be in a "search tips" link or "about Yahoo!," etc.)
28. Give out the student worksheet and assign each student three search engines to examine (from the list provided); include one of each type (but students will not know which search engine is which type). They must identify the type of search engine for each of their examples and then complete the chart for each search engine by exploring the links supplied on the search engine's Web site. This task can be done in pairs or individually.
29. Discuss the results with the class.

ARE THERE ANY PITFALLS OR POINTERS?

- Students may not know what *meta* means. Without giving it away, you may wish to supply a generic definition for that term.
- The card sets will be easier to separate and collect at the end of the session if each set is copied onto a different color of paper.
- Be sure to point out that with Yahoo! and other subject guides/directories it looks like the engine will be searching the Internet if the searcher types a word into the search box, but actually, it searches only within the subject guide/directory, not out on the "live" Internet.
- Also, point out that many of the "live" search engines look like a subject guide/directory at first glance because they have categories on their homepage as well. This is simply because categories have become a popular way to search. When you put a term into the search box in a "live" search engine, it goes out and searches the Internet, not a preselected database of Web sites, as the subject guide/directory does.
- Be aware that many search engines these days perform more than one function. For example, Google, as mentioned, functions as a subject guide/directory and as a "live" search engine. It will help your students if they know what to look for in the results list to determine how the search engine is functioning and therefore how the results have been obtained.

- Since Internet sites, including search engines, change so often, it will likely be necessary to update the list of search engines on the student handout quite regularly. You may also wish to use different examples should the ones suggested above change substantially. As we go to print, we are finding that Open Directory is a better example than Yahoo!, which has recently changed the way it displays its results.
- Some students may need extensive work on the search concepts (for example, Boolean oerators, wildcard/truncation, and so forth) prior to this activity.
- Because of differences in prior knowledge, some students may require individual help as they complete Support Material 19.
- In number 28 above, you may wish to assign the same search engines to each student or pair of students for ease of discussion later. Alternatively, the charts could be handed in for marking by the instructor.
- It is important to stress that any information from the Internet must be evaluated carefully. The benefits and drawbacks cards could mislead students into thinking that subject guide/directory sites have already been evaluated and the information is correct.

WHAT SAMPLES OR SUPPORT MATERIALS CAN I USE?

- Support Material 13: Search Engines Activity Worksheet—Instructor's Guide
- Support Material 14: Search Engines Worksheet—Student Handout (see CD-ROM)
  Note: For the above two worksheets, the instructions for accessing the library's Web page will need to be altered for your own library Web page.
- Support Material 15: Search Engines—Card Set 1—Types of Search Engines
- Support Material 16: Search Engines—Card Set 2—Definitions
- Support Material 17: Search Engines—Card Set 3—Benefits and Drawbacks (Some of these cards will need to be copied twice because they apply to more than one type of search engine. One card applies to all three. See support material for specific instructions.)
- Support Material 18: Search Engines—Benefits and Drawbacks Answer Key
- Support Material 19: Search Engine Guide (blank chart for students to fill in, with one example provided)

SUPPORT MATERIAL 13:
SEARCH ENGINES ACTIVITY

Instructor's Guide

TYPES OF SEARCH ENGINES

Subject guide/directory:

Organizes preselected Web sites into subject areas and allows users to click through a menu to find information on their topic. Using the search function of a subject guide/directory simply allows you to do a keyword search within the Web sites already organized by the subject guide/directory. Example: Yahoo!

"Live" search engine:

Performs a search by going out onto the World Wide Web and looking for Web sites that match the criteria you have asked for. This kind of search engine does not rely on sites it has already looked at for subject content, but will pick up any site on the Web that matches the search request. This kind of search will find new Web sites recently updated or published to the Web, as well as those that have been in existence for awhile. Example: Google

Metasearch engine:

Does a search by using the search function of several search engines at once. This kind of search engine will return the top five to ten results from each of a number of search engines. You are effectively searching with several search engines at once without having to go to each search engine individually. The downside of this kind of search engine is that it does a basic keyword search and is less likely to do sophisticated searching. Example: Metacrawler

EXERCISE

(These are the instructions the students have on their handout, Support Material 19.)

From the list of search engines below, you will be given three to examine. On the accompanying chart, provided by your instructor, you will be asked to fill in the following information:

- what kind of search engine each example is
- what kind of Boolean searching is supported
- what symbol represents the wildcard or truncation function for each search engine (it is often the asterisk [*] symbol)

continued on next page . . .

. . . continued from previous page

- whether the search engine will do "exact phrase" searching
- what advanced searching features exist, if any
- whether there are any other special features that add to the usefulness of the search engine

Subject Guides/Directories	"Live" Search Engines	Metasearch Engines
Yahoo! *www.yahoo.com* Looksmart *www.looksmart.com*	Northern Light *www.northernlight.com* AlltheWeb.com *www.alltheweb.com*	Metacrawler *www.metacrawler.com* Ask Jeeves *www.askjeeves.com* Dogpile *www.dogpile.com* Vivisimo *http://vivisimo.com*

Others:

Google (*www.google.com*)—functions as a subject guide/directory and a "live" search engine

AltaVista (*www.altavista.com*)—as above, subject guide/directory and "live" search engine

Excite (*www.excite.com*)—includes "live," subject guide/directory, and metasearch functions— searchers choose which function they would like to use

HotBot (*www.hotbot.com*)—subject guide/directory (if you click on the categories) and "live" search engine (if you perform a search in the search box)

Lycos (*www.lycos.com*)—connected with HotBot, for example, both are part of the "Lycos Network"—both a subject guide/directory and a "live" search engine

WHAT TO LOOK FOR WHEN EXAMINING SEARCH ENGINES

- Can you do a Boolean search? Does the search engine recognize the symbols + and – or do you need to use AND, OR, and NOT? Does it allow both?
- Does the search engine use the * symbol as a wildcard, or does it use something else instead?
- Can you do "exact phrase" searching in the search engine? That is, can you indicate that you would like to find a phrase (or idea that contains more than one word) with the words in the exact order they are written?
- Is there an advanced searching function? If so, what kinds of advanced searches can you do?
- What are the special features of the search engine? Does it do something interesting or unusual that other search engines do not? These special features could be related to how the information and search results are presented, speed of searching, quality of searching, and so forth.

SUPPORT MATERIAL 15:

SEARCH ENGINES—CARD SET 1—TYPES OF SEARCH ENGINES

Note: Support Materials 15–17 occur in larger format on the accompanying CD-ROM.

SUBJECT GUIDE/ DIRECTORY

"LIVE" SEARCH ENGINE

METASEARCH ENGINE

SUPPORT MATERIAL 16:

SEARCH ENGINES—CARD SET 2—DEFINITIONS

Subject Guide/Directory

- **This is an Internet "database" of Web sites.**

- **Web sites are chosen according to the subject of the site.**

- **This type of search engine does not search the Internet; it searches in its own database of pre-selected web sites.**

"Live" Search Engine

- **This search engine goes out onto the Internet to find the information you request.**

- **None of the information it finds has been evaluated by anyone working for the search engine.**

- **It will find the latest sites that have been published to the Internet.**

Metasearch Engine

- **This search engine uses other search engines to find results.**

- **This kind of search engine will always show you which search engines were used to find the results.**

SUPPORT MATERIAL 17:

SEARCH ENGINES—CARD SET 3—BENEFITS AND DRAWBACKS

Information found might not be up to date.

Search engine is good for finding up-to-date information.

Web sites have been chosen by search engine staff; therefore, the relevance should be better.

The sites found may not be that relevant—you need to evaluate them carefully.

The sites found may not be of high quality—you need to evaluate them carefully.

Search engine is less likely to provide an advanced search function.

You can use a simple or a very complex search string. You can control your searching better.

SUPPORT MATERIAL 18:

SEARCH ENGINES—BENEFITS AND DRAWBACKS ANSWER KEY

Note: The benefits/drawbacks that are listed in more than one place below should be duplicated accordingly from Support Material 17.

Subject Guide/ Directory	"Live" Search Engine	Metasearch Engine
Information found might not be up to date.	Search engine is good for finding up-to-date information.	Search engine is good for finding up-to-date information.
Web sites have been chosen by search engine staff; therefore, the relevance should be better.	The sites found may not be that relevant—you need to evaluate them carefully.	The sites found may not be that relevant—you need to evaluate them carefully.
The sites found may not be of high quality—you need to evaluate them carefully.	The sites found may not be of high quality—you need to evaluate them carefully.	The sites found may not be of high quality—you need to evaluate them carefully.
Can use both a simple or very complex search string. You can control your searching better.	You can use a simple or a very complex search string. You can control your searching better.	Search engine is less likely to provide an advanced search function.

SUPPORT MATERIAL 19:
SEARCH ENGINE GUIDE

Enter the names of the search engines you will be examining across the top of the chart. Explore each search engine to complete the table.

	Google			
Type of search engine	"Live" search engine			
AND	+, AND			
OR	OR			
NOT	-, NOT			
Wildcard/ truncation	Not available			
Exact phrase	"united states"			
Advanced searching	Yes: advanced search			
Other features	Search tips includes help with searching and FAQ (frequently asked questions)			

10

Evaluating Web Sites I

Now that your students are expert Internet searchers, they need to know how to separate the wheat from the chaff. This activity will introduce students to the main concepts and criteria necessary for evaluating Web sites.

WHAT WILL THE STUDENTS LEARN?

Students will be able to
- identify the parts of a Web site and the function of each part
- develop a list of criteria suitable for evaluating a Web site
- identify the parts of the Web site that would provide information relating to each criterion

HOW MUCH TIME WILL I NEED?

You will need 50 to 60 minutes.

WHAT PREPARATION OR MATERIALS ARE REQUIRED?

- suitable sample Web site, for example, *www.newyorktimes.com*
- Parts of a Web Site (card set)
- Criteria for Evaluating a Web Site—Headings (card set)
- Criteria for Evaluating a Web Site—Details (card set)
- Blu-Tak or similar adhesive putty for sticking cards to white board
- white board

HOW DOES IT WORK?

1. Ask the students how they currently evaluate a Web site (for example, how do you decide if a Web site is good for your research need?).

2. Display the suggested Web site *www.newyorktimes.com* (or use your own choice—see *Are There Any Pitfalls or Pointers?*).

Parts of a Web Site (blue cards)

3. Give out Parts of a Web Site cards (Support Material 20). Each person or group gets one or more cards.
4. Invite the students to come up and fix their cards onto the relevant parts on the Web site that is projected onto the screen (preferably a wall or white board).
   a) Alternatively, brainstorm the parts and write them on the board.
   b) All Web sites do not use the same terminology. Sometimes information about the site may be found under FAQ instead of About This Site.
5. Discuss to ensure that everyone understands what each part is and where to look for it on a Web site.

Criteria for Evaluating a Web Site (white and pink cards)

6. Put heading cards (white cards; Support Material 21—Useful/Not Useful for Evaluating as Academic Source) up on white board.

Figure 10–1. First put the heading cards at the top.

7. Give out pink cards. (Support Material 22—Criteria for Evaluating a Web Site—headings). Note: There are some "red herrings."
8. Ask the students to put the criteria (pink) cards under one of the headings (white cards) on the white board.

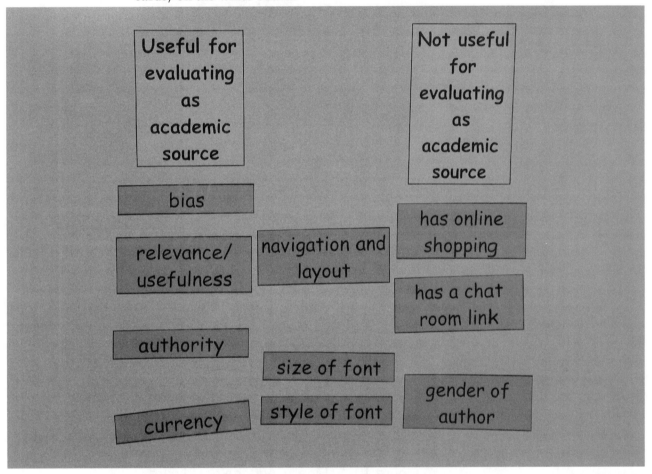

Figure 10–2. Now, add the criteria cards.

9. Discuss results:
   a) Some of the criteria relate to the design of the Web site, and although this is one aspect of evaluation, it is not one that we wish to emphasize because we are concentrating on evaluation of the site as a suitable academic source.
   b) The instructor should explain this and remove any criteria relating to design (for example, navigation and layout) for the next part of the lesson.
10. Take all cards off the board. Put the four main criteria cards back up along the top of the board with space beneath them. These four cards are authority, bias, currency, and relevance/usefulness (the order does not particularly matter).
11. Give out the next set of cards (yellow cards, Support Material 23—Criteria for Evaluating a Web Site—Details).
12. Ask the students to group the cards under the appropriate criteria headings. For example, "If I found a copyright date on the Web site, what might this help me evaluate?" (Answer: Currency.)

13. Discuss the results. Some cards may relate to more than one heading.

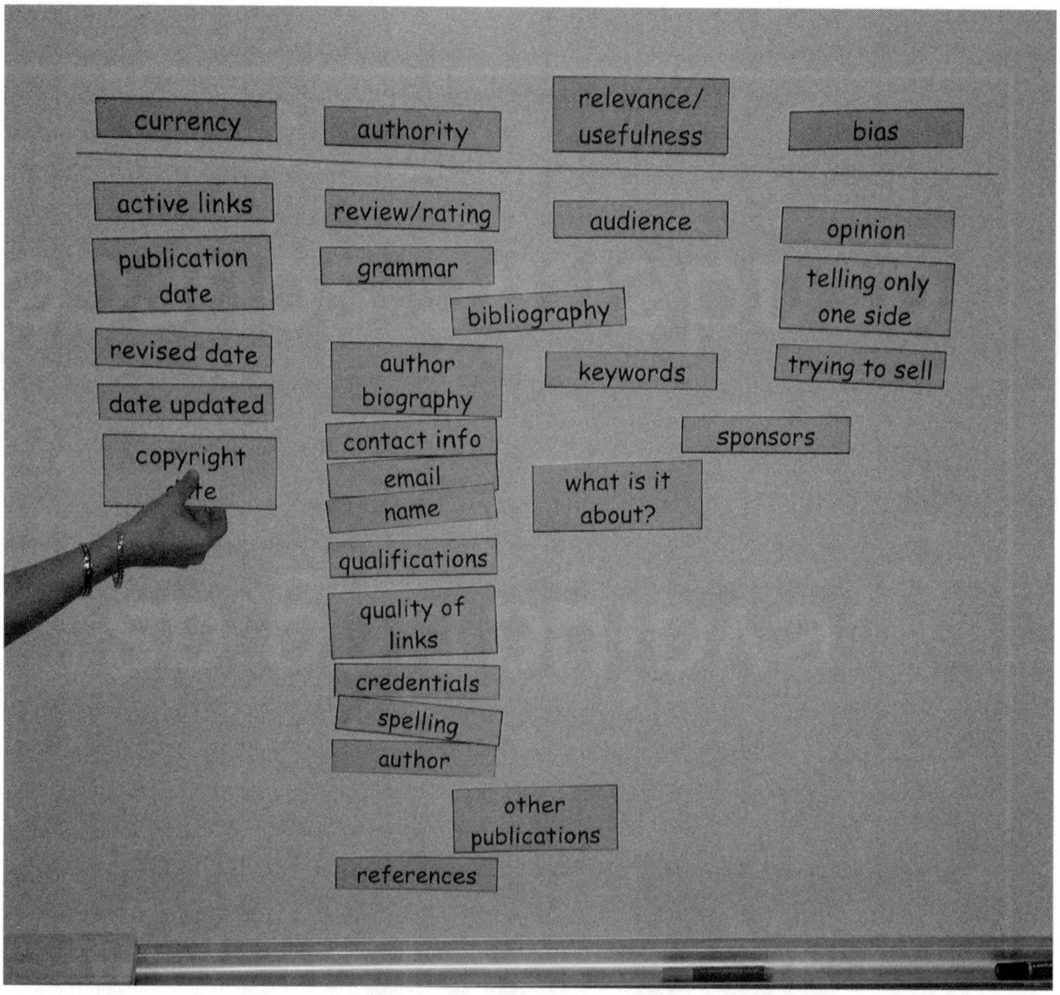

Figure 10–3. Finally, add the detail cards

Matching Worksheet

14. Give out Evaluating Web Sites Matching Activity (Support Material 24).
15. Direct the students to work in groups or pairs to come up with the places one would look for each of these criteria.
16. Discuss the results.

ARE THERE ANY PITFALLS OR POINTERS?

- We have suggested a site that presents a good example of the various parts of a Web site. There will be many other sites with the same criteria and you may wish to select your own sample site that has relevance to the content area that your students are studying or researching.

- WARNING: Any suggested Web sites should be previewed carefully by instructors before use. The transient nature of the Web means that sites that were recently excellent examples may have moved to another URL, may have been removed altogether, or may have changed in content and are no longer suitable for the activity or the class.
- ESL students may need to spend a session prior to this one becoming familiar with some of the vocabulary.
- Students usually need to be encouraged to explore the Web site more fully to uncover some of the information they need to evaluate the Web page. For instance, the author is sometimes listed only on the homepage of the site. Similarly, the date is often difficult to find. Information pertaining to the author's credentials and experience must also be hunted down. It is helpful if the instructor stresses this point when going over the Matching Activity Worksheet.

WHAT SAMPLES OR SUPPORT MATERIALS CAN I USE?

Four card sets (copy each card set in a different color for ease of sorting at the end of a session; then laminate):

- Support Material 20: Evaluating Web Sites I—Card Set 1—Parts of a Web Site (blue)
- Support Material 21: Evaluating Web Sites I—Card Set 2—Headings (white)
- Support Material 22: Evaluating Web Sites I—Card Set 3—Criteria for Evaluating a Web Site—Headings (pink)
- Support Material 23: Evaluating Web Sites I—Card Set 4—Criteria for Evaluating a Web Site—Details (yellow)
- Support Material 24: Evaluating Web Sites Matching Activity

SUPPORT MATERIAL 20:

EVALUATING WEB SITES I—CARD SET 1—PARTS OF A WEB SITE (DUPLICATE ON BLUE CARD)

Note: This is a sampling only; the full set can be found on the accompanying CD-ROM. In addition, this sample has been reduced in size and can be found in larger format on the CD-ROM.

homepage

graphics

URL

continued on next page . . .

. . . *continued from previous page*

"about this site"

body of the text

links

SUPPORT MATERIAL 21:
EVALUATING WEB SITES I—CARD SET 2—HEADINGS
(DUPLICATE ON WHITE CARD)

Note: The material is shown here in a reduced form; the original size can be found on the accompanying CD-ROM.

Useful for evaluating as academic source

continued on next page . . .

. . . *continued from previous page*

Not useful for

evaluating as

academic source

SUPPORT MATERIAL 22:

EVALUATING WEB SITES I—CARD SET 3—CRITERIA FOR EVALUATING A WEB SITE—HEADINGS (DUPLICATE ON PINK CARD)

Note: This is a sampling only; the full set can be found on the accompanying CD-ROM. In addition, the material is shown here in a reduced form; the original size can be found on the CD-ROM.

currency

bias

relevance/ usefulness

continued on next page . . .

. . . *continued from previous page*

authority

size of font

SUPPORT MATERIAL 23:
EVALUATING WEB SITES I—CARD SET 4—CRITERIA FOR EVALUATING A WEB SITE—DETAILS (DUPLICATE ON YELLOW CARD)

Note: This is a sampling only; the full set can be found on the accompanying CD-ROM. In addition, the material is shown here in a reduced form; the original size can be found on the CD-ROM.

what is it about?

opinion

group responsible

continued on next page . . .

. . . continued from previous page

publication date

author

credentials

SUPPORT MATERIAL 24: EVALUATING WEB SITES MATCHING ACTIVITY		
What do you look for:	**Where?**	**Choose from:**
Relevance/Usefulness • What it is about ◦ Keywords • Who the audience is		• Title • Body of the text
Currency • Updated date • Revised date • Copyright date • Active links (i.e., do they all work?)		• Graphics • URL • Bottom of the screen
Authority • Author ◦ name ◦ biography ◦ credentials/qualifications ◦ other publications ◦ group or organization responsible for the page • Bibliography • E-mail contact/ contact information • Quality of links (Are they good ones?) • Design elements (Does it look professional?) • Spelling and grammar (Are there mistakes?) • Reviews and ratings		• Homepage • "About this site" (might be included in FAQs or might have another name entirely) • Links provided in text or at end of page • Whole site
Bias • Trying to sell something? • Opinion? • Telling only part of the story? • Is there a sponsor (e.g., a company) who has a specific interest?		• Advertising

11

Evaluating Web Sites II

This practical activity will have your students evaluating actual Web sites, applying the concepts and criteria discovered in the previous session. It can be done in isolation, but is more effective as a follow-up to Evaluating Web Sites I (page 57).

WHAT WILL THE STUDENTS LEARN?

Students will apply the concepts and skills learned in the previous session by examining Web pages and evaluating them.

HOW MUCH TIME WILL I NEED?

You will need 30 minutes.

WHAT PREPARATION OR MATERIALS ARE REQUIRED?

- Evaluating Web Sites—Criteria Worksheet (two copies per student)
- List of Web Sites to Evaluate (Student Handout; two versions)
- List of Web Sites to Evaluate, with Annotations (Instructor Guide; two versions)

HOW DOES IT WORK?

1. Using the Instructor Guide (Support Material 25 or 27), display the first Web site listed and evaluate it through class discussion (the whole class, led by instructor), according to the criteria on the Evaluating Web Sites Worksheet (Support Material 29).
2. Repeat for the second listed Web site.
3. Use the teaching points on the Instructor Guide to direct the discussion.
4. After sufficient discussion, break the class into small groups, give out the student handout (Support Material 26 or 28), and assign each group two Web sites to examine.

Explain that they should use the Evaluating Web Sites worksheet and that they will be expected to explain their findings to the class.

5. Give the students ten minutes to complete this activity.
6. Ask each group to report their findings to the class. The instructor should facilitate the discussion and add points as needed.

ARE THERE ANY PITFALLS OR POINTERS?

- This session follows on from Evaluating Web Sites I (page 57), where students explored the criteria useful for evaluating a Web site or page and learned where to look for this information on any particular site or page.
- See *What Preparation or Materials Are Required?* (above): There are two versions of this activity. One looks at Web sites about Lady Diana and the other, Anastasia Romanov. For each, we have provided a student handout and accompanying instructor guide. Instructors may choose either of these or select their own Web sites as examples and apply the same evaluation criteria.
- Due to the changing nature of the Internet, the Web sites we have suggested may not be available at the same address or may have disappeared. If you cannot find these sites, feel free to substitute sites of your own.

WHAT SAMPLES OR SUPPORT MATERIALS CAN I USE?

- Support Material 25: List of Diana Web Sites, with Annotations—Instructor Guide
- Support Material 26: List of Diana Web Sites—Student Handout
- Support Material 27: List of Anastasia Web Sites, with Annotations—Instructor Guide (see CD-ROM)
- Support Material 28: List of Anastasia Web Sites—Student Handout (see CD-ROM)
- Support Material 29: Evaluating Web Sites—Criteria Worksheet (two copies per student)

SUPPORT MATERIAL 25: EVALUATING WEB SITES II

Instructor Guide

Use the two following examples for discussion with the class:

www.cnn.com/WORLD/9708/31/diana.links/

This is the CNN Web site on Diana. It looks authoritative enough, especially when the information is backed by other sources, but keep in mind that any news source could have some bias.

www.monash.com/diana.html

This site seems to satisfy most of the criteria, but when read, it becomes apparent that the content is biased and very personal; it was created by novelist Linda Barlow. Be sure to look at the list of her other publications (historical fiction/romance/mysteries). In addition, the design is a clue to the nature of the content—be sure to point out that watermarked pink Lady Dianas are an instant warning sign!

Sites for Students to Explore:

1. http://news.bbc.co.uk/hi/english/static/diana_one_year_on/default.stm

This is the BBC Diana page.

2. www.paralumun.com/diana.htm

This site could be all right, but there is absolutely no author information given, no list of sources used, or anything to indicate that the creator of the Web site didn't just make it up. (A good example to point students to is the Dodi link that includes obvious spelling and grammatical errors as well as hearsay information.)

3. www.geocities.com/CapitolHill/Congress/4333/

This material was written by a 17-year-old male. The grammar is bad, and the spelling too, but there is a lot of information. You can find out the author's name and e-mail him, but he has no particular authority to write this page. Also, there is the whole question of conspiracy theories. Researchers must give such sites a great deal of thought before accepting what is written.

Note: These URLs may not be correct due to the continually changing nature of the Internet. If you cannot find these sites, or if they no longer appear to be suitable, feel free to select sites of your own.

SUPPORT MATERIAL 26:
EVALUATING WEB SITES II

Student Handout

Look at the following Web sites. Evaluate them based on the checklist you have received. Which ones are good sites to use for a research project on Princess Diana and her life?

1. *http://news.bbc.co.uk/hi/english/static/diana_one_year_on/default.stm*

2. *www.paralumun.com/diana.htm*

3. *www.geocities.com/CapitolHill/Congress/4333/*

SUPPORT MATERIAL 29:
EVALUATING WEB SITES—CRITERIA WORKSHEET

Title of Web site/page/article: _____

URL: _____

Criteria	Your Evaluation
Relevant/Useful? • How might the information on the page be useful for your project?	
Current/Up to Date? • Is the information on the page current? (What is the date? It could say updated on or revised on.) • Does it matter for your particular topic?	
Authoritative? • Who is the author?	
• What does the author tell you about himself? • Why do you feel the author is knowledgeable about the topic? (Look for his credentials or experience.) • Has he published other books or papers on the topic?	
• What group is responsible for the Web site other than the author? (Is it a government body? A company? An educational institution? A research institution? An individual? Other?)	

Your overall evaluation of the site:

• Strengths: _____

• Weaknesses: _____

12

Databases I

This highly interactive activity is very effective for making concrete the abstract concept of a database. It is also a lot of fun!

WHAT WILL THE STUDENTS LEARN?

Students will learn what a database is and how it organizes information for ease of searching.

HOW MUCH TIME WILL I NEED?

You will need 30 minutes.

WHAT PREPARATION OR MATERIALS ARE REQUIRED?

- laminated articles (full, not cut into parts)
  - The number of articles chosen will be determined by the number of students typically attending a session. It is best if no more than three students are working on one article.
- laminated articles (cut into parts)
- laminated blank strips (three per article)
- laminated field headings
- white board markers
- white board eraser(s)
- white board
- bulldog clips
- table or large flat area upon which the database can be "built"
- telephone book

HOW DOES IT WORK?

Summary:

After discussion of the different parts of an article (such as, "fields" in a database), students apply subject headings to an article that they have been given and arrange the parts of the article under the appropriate field headings. All the articles together, organized in this way with the addition of subject headings, create a mini-database that can be used to discuss the concept of a database and to demonstrate the effectiveness of field searching.

1. Put laminated articles on the walls at the front of the classroom for students to view.
2. Invite the students to come to the front and look at the articles.
3. Ask the class:
   a) What are these? (Answer: Articles.)
   b) Where do they come from? (Answer: Periodicals—magazines, journals, and newspapers.)
   c) What are they generally about? (Answer: If you do not have a theme, the answer will be "all subjects.")
   d) Can you find an article about _____?
   e) Can you find an article about _____? (For these two questions, the students will have to scan the articles on the wall to find the one you are asking for. This should take them awhile, but sometimes by chance a student will see it right away. For this reason, it is good to ask them at least twice to find an article. These questions are designed to highlight how long it takes to find information this way and, in some cases, the students may not find what they are looking for at all.)
4. Ask the students to take the articles off the wall and back to their seat. (They can do this in pairs; it depends on the ratio of the number of students to the number of articles.)
5. Ask the students to identify the different parts of their article. Give them an example to start with, such as, the title (write **title** on the board). As they provide answers, write these on the board to create a list of article parts. (You are looking for at least:
   a) title
   b) author
   c) abstract
   d) source
   e) date
   f) full text

   and sometimes students will add "subject," but not always. If they do not, don't try to elicit it here. If they give you more than this, that is all right; usually you can demonstrate how these extras fit into one of the above categories. For example, "volume number" could fit into source, "introduction" could fit into full text.)
6. Once you have a list that includes all of the above words (with the possible exception of *subject*), pick up one of the cut-up articles and explain that you'll be giving them a packet like this, which will be their article cut up into the parts you have just talked about.
7. Do not give the packets out yet. The following should be done on a large flat area (a

table or the floor) big enough to hold all the headings cards, with all the students' article parts organized underneath them. See Figure 12–1 for a visual of how the table should look at the beginning of this activity.

a) Explain that the students will need to figure out which part is the title of their article (hold up the *title* field heading card) and put it below this heading (place the card on the table with room beneath it for the students' article titles).

b) "The author of your article will go underneath the author heading" (place the *author* card on the table), and so forth.

c) Do all except the subject card.

8. Show the students that included in their cut-up article packet are three strips identified with the title of their article. Explain that they will need to read their article, determine what it is about, think of three keywords that reflect what their article is about (for example, children, public schools, advertising), and write each keyword on one of the three strips. (Note: Students may feel inclined to write whole sentences. Stress that there should only be one or two words per strip.)

9. Explain that they will then need to place these strips underneath the *subject* card on the table (hold up the card with *subject* on it and put it on the table with the others).

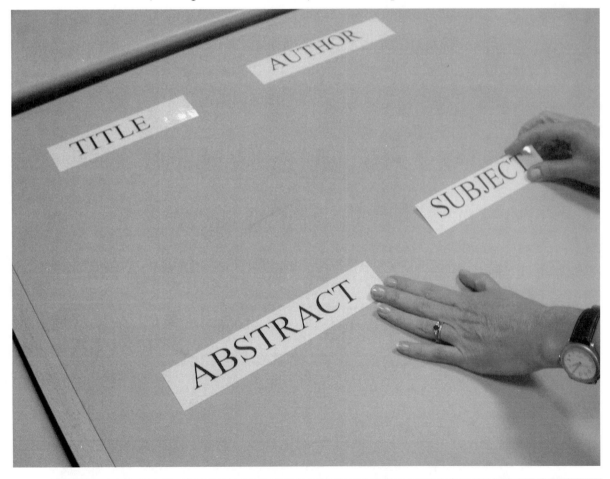

Figure 12–1. Headings are shown on table/flat surface (no parts of articles down yet).

10. Check for comprehension by asking:
    a) What will you do first? (Answer: Read the article.)
    b) What will you do next? (Answer: Decide the keywords and put them on the strips.)
    c) What will you do last? (Answer: Put parts of the articles, including the keywords, underneath the appropriate headings on the table or floor.)
    (See Figure 10 for how the table should look after the students have completed this activity.)

11. Give the students time to do this. Walk around and help out, especially with the keywords, as they often find this difficult. Steer them toward one- and two-word ideas. This undertaking will be more difficult for second-language learners than for native speakers of English. You may need to supervise the placing of article parts under the headings on the table and correct any mistakes as they happen. (You may also wish to guide the students who have the articles you discussed in number 3 by asking them to use a keyword approximating what you asked them to find earlier. That is, if you asked them, "Can you find an article about advertising?" you will want to ensure that the student who has that article uses *advertising* or *advertisements* on at least one of the keyword strips.)

12. Ask the class to gather around the table when everyone is finished and all the articles have been arranged underneath the appropriate headings. Explain to them that they have just built a database.

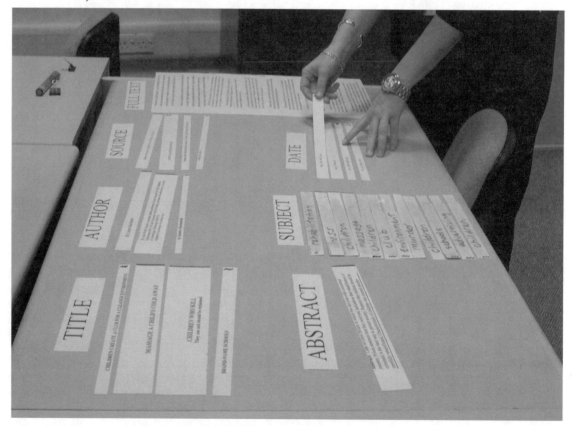

Figure 12–2. Headings with parts of articles arranged underneath

13. Repeat the two (or more) questions you asked above in number 3: Can you find an article about _____ ? (It is important to ask the same two (or more) questions you did earlier since this will illustrate how much more quickly you can find information in a database than by simply browsing.) The students will probably hesitate at first, but someone will realize that they should look at the subject keywords to find the article most quickly. After that, they will all get the idea.

Ask them:
   a)   Was that easier than when I asked you the same questions before? (Answer: Yes.)
   b)   Why? What did we do to the information to make it easier to find? (Answer: We cut it up into parts and added subjects.)

Ask the question Can you find an article about _____? several more times, using keywords that the students have placed on the table. To make the activity more realistic, it is helpful, after the first few examples, to use synonyms of the keywords the students have used. For instance, if a student wrote *murder*, you could ask if they can find an article about *homicide* (higher level) or *killing* (lower level). This approach starts students thinking about how the search terms in a database may or may not match their own way of describing a topic.

Other questions to ask:
   a)   How many articles were written in ___(year)___?
   b)   Is there an article written by _____? (Check ahead of time for a name to use.)
   c)   Can you find an article published in the *Journal of* _____?
   d)   Use any other questions that will help to illustrate how field searching works and how quickly you can find seemingly obscure information easily in a database.

14. Show the class a phone book. Explain that this is a database too. Ask:
   a)   How is the information organized in this database? How do you find it? (Answer: By name.)
   b)   If I had a phone number and wanted to know which name belonged to the phone number, could I look it up in here? (Answer: No, it would be nearly impossible.)
   c)   What if I cut up the information in the phone book as we have done today?" (Answer: Yes, that would work; however, it would still be a very time consuming task.)
   d)   What if I cut up the phone book and then put the information into a computer? (Answer: That would work well.)

15. Explain that the electronic databases on our library Web page are just like this database that we've made. Ask:
   a)   Who chose these articles? (Answer: You/instructor.)
   b)   What did I base my decisions on? (Answer: The subject, if a theme is used; the quality of the articles.)
   c)   Who chose the subjects in our database? (Answer: We did/students.)
   d)   What did you base your decisions on? (Answer: What the article was about.)

Explain about quality control in a commercial database. For less advanced audiences, you can use the idea of an editor, accepting good articles and rejecting bad ones. For more advanced audiences who have English as their first language, you can explain that each database includes articles from certain publications and the editors of those publications are technically the quality control managers for the database because the database accepts all articles published in those sources.

Explain about subject headings in commercial databases. Database companies hire people to decide what subject(s) each article is about. Like the students, they base their decisions on what the article is about, but they also try to take into account how people might try to access this information. (Use an illustration—and this is best if it comes from the their own keywords from this activity—the murder/homicide/killing example. They quickly see that different people think of a topic in different ways and that deciding which subject heading to use is trickier than it first appears.)

Drive home the point that this is why we ask them to do brainstorming at the beginning of the process. (See Brainstorming Your Search Terms, page 35.) If they have a big list of words to search with, then differences in terminology won't stump them as much.

16. Show the students one of the library's electronic databases and indicate the fields— just like in "our" database.

ARE THERE ANY PITFALLS OR POINTERS?

- This is the first activity in a group of database activities that go together.
- See Databases II (page 89) for the next activity in the sequence.
- Instructors will have to choose their own articles according to the language level of their students. Be sure to include articles that have clearly identifiable fields, such as, title, author, abstract, source, date, and so forth. (See Support Material 31 for an example of the kinds of articles to use.) In addition, it is helpful to choose a number of articles on the same theme, but this is not absolutely necessary. The number of articles chosen will be determined by the number of students typically attending a session. No more than three students should be working on the same article.
- Practical hint: The students should write their keywords onto the blank strips using white board markers so they can be easily erased afterward. Ask the students to erase their keyword strips and put their article back together after the activity is over. It is time consuming to attempt this task by yourself after each session!
- In order to keep each cut-up article together and not mix up the pieces, it is best if each part of the same article (including the blank strips) has a symbol on it (preferably added before laminating so it will not rub off later). For instance, one article might have all its pieces identified with a star, another with a triangle, and another with a circle. This labeling serves two purposes: a) it becomes easy to put each article together again after the activity is over, and b) it is easy for the students to see which keyword goes with which article (once the sample database has been built and is spread out on the table or floor)—it mimics the internal coding in a database that links the parts together. Alternately, each cut-up article could be photocopied on different colored paper.

WHAT SAMPLES OR SUPPORT MATERIALS CAN I USE?

- Support Material 30: Field Headings Cards
- Support Material 31: Sample Article. (Instructors should select their own from periodical databases that their institution subscribes to (see *Are There Any Pitfalls or Pointers?*) Enlarge articles to A3/11"x 17" size, photocopy twice, laminate both sets, and cut up one set into the various parts mentioned in the instructions above.)
- Support Material 32: Blank Strips (You need three strips per article. Laminate.)

SUPPORT MATERIAL 30:
DATABASES I—FIELD HEADINGS

Note: This material is included in larger format on the accompanying CD-ROM.

TITLE

AUTHOR

SOURCE

DATE

ABSTRACT

FULL TEXT

SUBJECT

SUPPORT MATERIAL 31:
DATABASES I—SAMPLE ARTICLE

HEALTHY FOOD FOR SCHOOL-AGE CHILDREN

Abstract: Briefly outlines the importance of nutritional lunches for school children and provides suggestions for what to put into the lunch box.

Many children today spend hours at school fueled by insufficient and unhealthy foods. For maximum nutrition and to help children concentrate, each of the following food groups should be included in every meal.

Bread, Cereal, Rice, and Pasta Group

These foods are very important as they provide energy as well as important fiber. Examples include: breads and rolls, muffins, pita bread, or a small container of leftover rice or pasta (which can be served cold).

Fruit Group

These are easy to pack and essential for important vitamins, minerals, and carbohydrates for energy. Some of the usual favorites are apples, oranges, mandarins, and bananas, but other fruits such as rock melon, watermelon, and peaches can be cut into small pieces and put into a plastic container.

Vegetable Group

Vegetables are also important for vitamin and mineral content as well as added fiber. Some that are popular with children are corn, small cucumbers, green beans, carrot sticks, peas, and snow peas. Most of these are enjoyed raw.

Meat, Fish, Poultry, Eggs, and Nut Group

These foods provide protein that builds muscle. Cold sliced meats and chicken breast meat or drumsticks can all be part of a healthy lunch. Tuna sandwiches have long been a healthy favorite and a boiled egg or a handful of nuts is also popular (although be wary of nuts with younger children).

continued on next page . . .

. . . continued from previous page

Milk, Yogurt, and Cheese

These foods provide more vitamins and minerals and help bones to grow strong. Most children enjoy a plain or flavored milk, yogurt, or sliced cheese—all easy additions to the lunch box.

With a little thought and planning your child can benefit from a healthy and balanced diet which will support the growth and learning process.

By Pamela Robertson

"Healthy Food for School Age Children" is the property of Healthweek and may not be copied without the copyright holder's express written permission.

Healthweek, Vol. 45 Issue 7, p. 78

Nov. 26, 2001

SUPPORT MATERIAL 32:
DATABASES I—BLANK STRIPS

Note: This material can be customized by using the version included on the accompanying CD-ROM.

(Title of article goes here)

(Title of article goes here)

(Title of article goes here)

(Title of article goes here)

(Title of article goes here)

13

Databases II

Now that your students understand what a database is, you can use this simulation to demonstrate how a computer searches for information in a database. This activity can be used on its own, but is a natural extension of Databases I (page 77–88).

WHAT WILL THE STUDENTS LEARN?

Students will learn how a database searches, including the difference between keyword and subject (or field) searching and how Boolean operators function.

HOW MUCH TIME WILL I NEED?

You will need 30 minutes.

WHAT PREPARATION OR MATERIALS ARE REQUIRED?

- laminated articles with highlighted keywords (five or six sets of nine articles each)
- Boolean Frogs and Fish (five or six sets) (page 97) or Boolean Attribute Shapes (see CD-ROM)

HOW DOES IT WORK?

Part 1: Keyword versus Subject Searching

1. Hand out the sets of articles (Support Material 33)—one per group of students (no more than three students per group).
2. Explain that the students will be the computer and you (the instructor) will be the searcher.
3. Draw a computer screen on the board (or just write on the board, as you like) and write the word **China** inside the screen.

4. Tell the students you'd like articles about China. Explain that as computers, they will search every article in their packet for the word **China** and pull out those articles that contain the word. (All search terms are highlighted to facilitate ease of searching.)

5. Give the students time to do this. Ask them how many articles they found. (Answer: Four.) Ask if all the articles are about **China** (the country). Go through them one by one and discuss what each one is about (quickly). One article is about porcelain china. Ask the class why they found this article. (Answer: Because it contained the word **china** and the computer does not discriminate.)

6. Erase **China** and write **school**. Ask the students to search for this new term.

7. Ask them how many articles they found. (Answer: Two.)
   Note: Many students will find three since they will pick out the article "Home Schooling." This article contains the words **schools** and **schooling** but not **school** so it does not actually match the search criteria and would not be identified by a computer. Point out that the students are thinking and making connections like humans, and so they selected this article, but a computer cannot think and can only follow instructions and therefore would not select this article. Ask those who selected the "Home Schooling" article to put it back, as the computer would not find it, then ask the students to look quickly at the articles. Are all the articles about school? Go through them, quickly, discussing the subject of each article. One is about Pavarotti. Ask the class why they selected it. (Answer: Because the word **school** was mentioned.)

8. Point out that we have an article about **school** called "Home Schooling" that the computer did not find. Ask how we could change our search to make sure that the computer selected this article.

9. Write the wildcard or truncation symbol * on the board and ask if anyone knows what this is or how it works when searching.

10. Explain that this symbol commands the computer to search for the root of a word or the base of a word and all possible endings. For example: **school*** will make the computer search for **school, schools, schooling,** and so forth.

11. Ask students to search for **school***. Ensure that they now have the "Home Schooling" article as well as the others. (Students should have three articles now.)

12. Highlight the fact that we have done two searches, both of which found relevant and irrelevant articles. In addition, the computer missed an important article. Ask the students how we can change our search so that more relevant articles are found. (The students will likely suggest adding a word so that the search is more specific. Demonstrate this on the board by adding the word they suggest and connecting it with AND to the original search term.)

13. Explain that this is one good way, but there are also other ways to make their search more specific and relevant. Point out that there are parts to each article (title, author, source, abstract, text, and subject). Direct their attention to the subject field.

14. Ask the students "What would happen if I changed my search request from simply **China** to **SUBJECT: China**?" Where would they, as computers, look for the word? (Answer: In the subject field.) Ask them to do this new search. Look at the results. (Answer: Three.) The only articles they should have found are the ones with **China** in the subject field.

15. Erase **SUBJECT: China** and write **SUBJECT: schools**. How many articles do they get? (Answer: Two.) Are they both about schools? (Answer: Yes.)

16. Explain that the first way of searching was called Keyword searching. Elicit from the students what this means in terms of how the computer searches. (Answer: It looks in all fields for the term that has been typed into the search screen.)

17. Explain that the second way of searching was called Subject searching. Elicit from the students what this means in terms of how the computer searches. (Answer: It looks only in the subject field for the term typed into the search screen.)

18. At this point, the instructor could refer to the previous session (Databases I, page 77) and remind the students that subjects are added by a person as opposed to the computer. (In Databases I they actually had to read each article in order to create subject headings.) Therefore, because there are several ways to describe a topic, the subject headings will sometimes use terms that the students might not have thought of. This leads naturally into the technique of doing a keyword search first, and then looking at the subject headings of the articles that were found to see what terms are used to describe the articles in order to find further, more relevant articles.

19. Go on to refine these definitions if you wish, depending on the language level and sophistication of your audience. (Keyword searching is actually possible in any field. It simply means that the computer looks for the requested word anywhere within that field. So, we could have **subject keyword searching, title keyword searching,** etc. What we have done with the students above is actually **general keyword searching** and **subject keyword searching.** General keyword searches scan the whole record in the database; subject keyword searches scan only the subject field of the record.)

Part 2: Boolean Operators

1. Ask the students to do all of the following searches, pausing after each one to ask how many articles they found in their packets. (Write that number on the board next to the search terms.) You will end up with a list of searches, each with a number beside it.
   a) **china OR food** (7. You may need to clarify with them before they start searching that the OR means they will be looking for articles that contain only **China,** articles that contain only **food,** and articles that contain **both** words.)
   b) **china AND food** (2. Look only for articles that contain both words.)
   c) **land OR environment** (3)
   d) **land AND environment** (1)
   e) **food** (5)
   f) **SUBJECT: food** (4)
   g) **SUBJECT: food NOT nutrition** (3)
   h) **italy** (1)
   i) **ital*** (2)
   Note: Notice that we have not used capitals for the keywords above because computer searching is generally not case sensitive unless specifically stated.

2. Direct the students' attention to the searches written on the board, with the numbers beside them, and ask:
   a) What happens when you use OR? Does it make the search broader or narrower? (Answer: The search is broader.)
   b) What happens when you use AND? (Answer: The search is narrower.)
   c) What happens when you use NOT? (Answer: The search is narrower.)

    d)   What happens when you do a subject search? (Answer: The search is narrower.)

3. Give out the Boolean Frogs and Fish sets (Support Material 34, page 101)—one to each group of two or three students. Alternatively, use Boolean Attribute Shapes (Support Material 35, see CD-ROM) and follow the instructions for that activity. (See Boolean Frogs and Fish, page 97, for complete instructions for this activity.)

4. Draw two interlocking circles on the board. Indicate the one on the left and say that all the articles about frogs are in this circle (write **frogs** above the circle). Indicate the right-hand circle and say that all the articles about fish are in this circle (write **fish** above the circle).

5. Explain that each disk in their set of frogs and fish represents an article and the picture on the disk is the subject of the article.

6. Ask the students to put the disks into the circles.

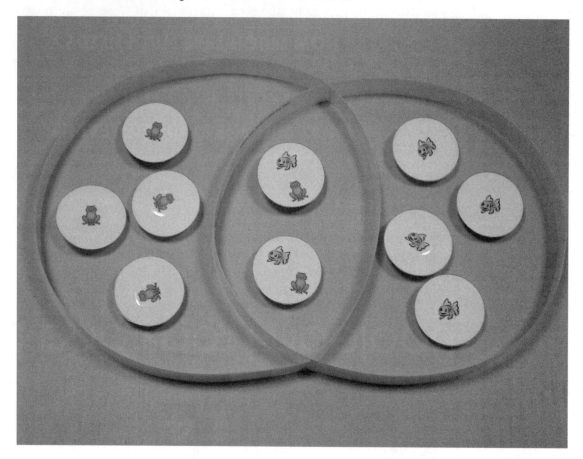

Figure 13–1. This students' set shows interlocking rings with discs in them.

7. Give the students time to do this and then ask them to tell you how to organize your own disks (magnetic) on the board in the circles you've drawn. (You can usually see, as they are arranging their own disks, if they've understood or not. They are usually very quick at doing this.)

8. Once you have put the disks in the correct places on the board under the students' direction, discuss any errors that may have occurred.

Figure 13–2. This instructor's set shows whiteboard with discs in circles.

9. Write the word **AND** between the words **frogs** and **fish** (written above the circles earlier). Ask the students which articles we would find if this were our search. (Answer: The ones in the interlocking part of the two circles.)

10. Erase **AND** and write **OR**. Ask the students which articles we would find now. (Answer: All of them.)

11. Erase **OR** and write **NOT**. Ask the students which articles we would find now. (Answer: Only the articles with frogs—the whole circle with **fish** in it, including the articles with both **frogs** and **fish**, will be excluded.)

12. Finally, add the red fish to the circle labeled **fish**. Write the following search on the board: **fish NOT red**. Ask how many articles we would find. (This is a little tricky for some students. They must include all articles that have **fish**, that is, the whole **fish** circle, but exclude the red fish.)

13. Make sure that they understand that using AND tells the computer it must find both words in the article for the article to satisfy the search. Using OR means that either word (or both) can be in the article. Using NOT means that the computer will exclude all articles that mention the word that comes after NOT.

14. Ask the class if they can think of a real-life searching situation when they might use OR. (Answer: Between synonyms and related terms.) Point out that on the Brain-

storming Your Search Terms worksheet (Support Material 11, page 39), used earlier in the course, words that were in the same bubble would be joined by OR. Words in different bubbles would be joined by AND.

15. Ask the students if they can think of a real-life situation when they might use NOT. (Answer: When you don't want a word to appear in your results.) A practical example is when you're searching for things about spiders, for instance. The concept of a spider's web often brings up information about the World Wide Web or the Internet. **spider web* NOT Internet** is an example of a NOT Boolean search. Another example, especially for more advanced classes, is a search on the term "literature review," as in the presearch a graduate student does to determine the amount of research already conducted on his topic. An actual search on these words turned up a journal named *The Rocky Mountain Literature Review*. Using **NOT literature review** in the journal field helped to solve this problem.

ARE THERE ANY PITFALLS OR POINTERS?

- This is the second activity in a group of database activities that go together.
- See Databases I (page 77) for the first activity in the sequence.
- Please note that the database articles provided below have been written specifically for this activity. The content of the articles is basically irrelevant and the authors and sources have been fabricated; the aim is solely to provide a structured way of looking at how a computer searches. Instructors should feel free to write their own articles or select articles from existing databases.
- The Boolean Frogs and Fish activity can be used prior to beginning the Boolean searches (the first step in Part 2) to introduce the concept and function of Boolean operators or after doing the Boolean searches (where it is currently placed in the instructions) to confirm and consolidate the concept of Boolean searching. Instructors should feel free to try it both ways and see which works better for them.
- The Boolean Attribute Shapes activity (page 103) can easily be used instead of the Boolean Frogs and Fish activity. The function of these two activities is identical and the Attribute Shapes activity may be easier to manage with a larger class.

WHAT SAMPLES OR SUPPORT MATERIALS CAN I USE?

- Support Material 33: Articles (Enlarge to A3/11"x17" size and laminate. Make five to six copies of each and put into sets so that each set contains all the articles. Highlight the keywords in yellow [before laminating] so that students will not be overwhelmed by the text in each article.)
- List of keywords to highlight in these articles:

land	Italy	Italy's	Italian
environment	china	nutrition	school
schools	schooling	food	

The following are separate activities:
- Support Material 34: Boolean Frogs and Fish Activity (page 101)
- Support Material 35: Boolean Attribute Shapes Activity (see CD-ROM)

SUPPORT MATERIAL 33:
DATABASES II—ARTICLES

Note: The first article has been included below. For the rest, see the accompanying CD-ROM.

Chinese food is best

By Charlotte Leung

Source: Nutrition Today, Vol. 14, no. 2, February 2001, p. 56

Abstract: The Chinese diet contains many exotic ingredients, which provide particular health benefits.

Chinese food is best

For centuries, the diet in China has contained special ingredients designed to keep the society healthy. Ginger is used in many Chinese recipes and as well as adding wonderful flavor, ginger is well known as a digestive aid. It is used to settle the stomach and prevent motion sickness.

Dried mushrooms are believed to help in lowering blood pressure and are a common ingredient in soups and many stir-fried dishes.

Certain types of chrysanthemum are used in Chinese cooking and are believed to rid the body of fevers. It is sometimes served as chrysanthemum tea or used in soup.

If you are suffering from a cough, then Chinese dried figs may help, as they are believed to moisten the lungs.

SUBJECTS:

China — food

Nutrition

14

Boolean Frogs and Fish

Here's another activity that renders an abstract concept concrete. Although it seems child-like, this activity is very effective. It can stand alone, but notice that it also makes up a part of Databases II (page 89).

WHAT WILL THE STUDENTS LEARN?

Students will understand the concept of Boolean logic and its application in the search process.

HOW MUCH TIME WILL I NEED?

You will need 5 to 10 minutes. (It should be done quickly.)

WHAT PREPARATION OR MATERIALS ARE REQUIRED?

- students' sets: disks with frogs and fish on them, interlocking rings (see Figure 13)
- teacher's set (optional): magnetized disks for demonstrating on the white board, including one red fish (see Figure 14)

HOW DOES IT WORK?

1. Give out the Boolean Frogs and Fish sets (Support Material 34, page 101)—one to each group of two or three students.
2. Draw two interlocking circles on the board. Indicate the one on the left and say that all the articles about frogs are in this circle (write **frogs** above the circle). Indicate the right-hand circle and say that all the articles about fish are in this circle (write **fish** above the circle).
3. Explain that each disk in their set of frogs and fish represents an article and the picture on the disk is the subject of the article.

4. Ask the students to put the disks into the circles.

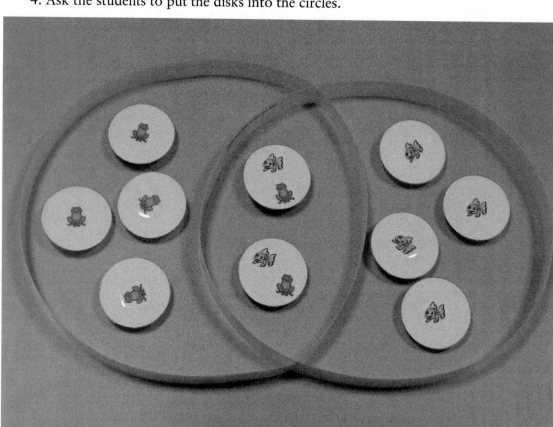

Figure 14–1. This students' set shows interlocking rings with discs in them.

5. Give the students time to do this and then ask them to tell you how to organize your own disks (magnetic) on the board in the circles you've drawn. (You can usually see, as they are arranging their own disks, if they've understood or not. They are usually very quick at doing this.)
6. Once you have put the disks in the correct places on the board under the students' direction, discuss any errors that may have occurred.

Figure 14–2. This instructor's set shows whiteboard with discs in circles.

7. Write the word **AND** between the words **frogs** and **fish** (written above the circles earlier). Ask the students which articles we would find if this were our search. (Answer: The ones in the interlocking part of the two circles.)

8. Erase **AND** and write **OR**. Ask the students which articles we would find now. (Answer: All of them.)

9. Erase **OR** and write **NOT**. Ask the students which articles we would find now. (Answer: Only the articles with frogs—the whole circle with **fish** in it, including the articles with both **frogs** and **fish,** will be excluded.)

10. Finally, add the red fish to the circle labeled **fish**. Write the following search on the board: **fish NOT red**. Ask how many articles we would find. (This is a little tricky for some students. They must include all articles that have fish—that is, the whole **fish** circle—but exclude the red fish.)

11. Make sure that they understand that using AND tells the computer it must find both words in the article for the article to satisfy the search. Using OR means that either word (or both) can be in the article. Using NOT means that the computer will exclude all articles that mention the word that comes after NOT.

12. Ask the class if they can think of a real-life searching situation when they might use OR. (Answer: Between synonyms and related terms.) Point out that on the Brain-

storming Your Search Terms worksheet (Support Material 11, page 39), used earlier in the course, words that were in the same bubble would be joined by OR. Words in different bubbles would be joined by AND.

13. Ask the students if they can think of a real-life situation when they might use NOT. (Answer: When you don't want a word to appear in your results.) A practical example is when you're searching for things about spiders, for instance. The concept of a spider's web often brings up information about the World Wide Web or the Internet. **spider web* NOT Internet** is an example of a NOT Boolean search. Another example, especially for more sophisticated classes, is a search on the term "literature review," as in the presearch a graduate student does to determine the amount of research already conducted on his topic. An actual search on these words turned up a journal named *The Rocky Mountain Literature Review*. Using **NOT literature review** in the journal field helped to solve this problem.

ARE THERE ANY PITFALLS OR POINTERS?

- This activity is best used with Databases II: Simulated Searching (page 89).
- This activity may be used as an alternative to Boolean Attribute Shapes (page 103).
- Sets should be made from cardboard (as per support material) and laminated to ensure long life.

WHAT SAMPLES OR SUPPORT MATERIALS CAN I USE?

- Support Material 34: Boolean Frogs and Fish
  ○ Disk with frog (You need four per set. Laminate.)
  ○ Disk with fish (You need four per set. Laminate.)
  ○ Disk with frog and fish (You need two per set. Laminate.)
  ○ Strips for making interlocking hoops (You need two per set. Laminate and assemble.)

(It's best to have one set for every two to three students. One set includes four frogs, four fish, and two disks with both frog and fish. In addition, each set needs one pair of interlocking rings. You will also need one instructor's set, which is exactly the same as the students' set, but includes a red fish [copy an extra fish disk and color it red]. Thus the instructor's set will have five fish, one of which is red. All instructor's disks should be put on magnets. Interlocking rings are not necessary because the instructor's version can be drawn on the board.)

SUPPORT MATERIAL 34:
BOOLEAN FROGS AND FISH

Strip for making interlocking hoops
(cut strip at dotted lines)

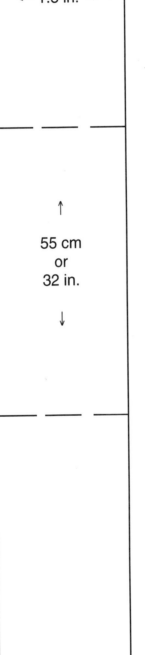

← 3.5 cm →
or
← 1.5 in. →

← 3.5 cm →
or
← 1.5 in. →

↑
55 cm
or
32 in.
↓

↑
55 cm
or
32 in.
↓

15

Boolean Attribute Shapes

While the concepts explored are the same as those in the previous activity, Boolean Attribute Shapes works well for larger groups. It can also be used as a follow-up to Boolean Frogs and Fish (page 97), and vice versa, to make sure the concept has been fully understood.

WHAT WILL THE STUDENTS LEARN?

Students will understand the concept of Boolean logic and its application in the search process.

HOW MUCH TIME WILL I NEED?

You will need 5 to 10 minutes.

WHAT PREPARATION OR MATERIALS ARE REQUIRED?

- set of attribute shapes (as per support material) copied in four different colors (include pink, blue, yellow, and green)

HOW DOES IT WORK?

1. Hand out between two and five shapes per student (depending on class size).
2. Explain that each shape represents an article that we are searching for and the attributes (such as, shape, color, and size) represent the criteria we can search by.
3. Say to the students:
   a) I am searching for **pink**. (Write **pink** on the board.) How many shapes match my search criteria?

     b)   All students with a pink shape hold it up to be counted. (The number should be recorded on the board beside the search term.)

     c)   I am searching for **pink AND round**. (Write the new search string under the previous one.)

     d)   How many shapes match my search criteria?

     e)   All students with a round pink shape hold it up to be counted. (Once again record the answer on the board beside that particular search string.)

     f)   What happened to the results? (Answer: There are fewer.)

     g)   What did the AND do to the search? (Answer: AND narrowed it.)

     h)   Why? (Answer: We were more specific or we had two criteria that both needed to be met to make a match.)

4. Repeat the process to consolidate the concept (again writing the bolded search terms on the board). Say to the students:

     a)   I am searching for **yellow**. How many shapes match my search criteria? (Write the number next to the search term on the board.)

     b)   I am searching for **yellow AND square**. How many shapes match my search criteria now? (Once again record the answer on the board beside that particular search string.)

     c)   What happened to the results? (Answer: There are fewer.)

     d)   What did the AND do to the search? (Answer: AND narrowed it.)

     e)   Why? (Answer: We were more specific or we had two criteria that both needed to be met to make a match.)

5. Say to the students (and write the bolded search words on the board):

     a)   I am searching for **blue**. How many shapes match my search criteria?

     b)   All students with a blue shape hold it up to be counted. (Record the number.)

     c)   I am searching for **blue OR green**. How many shapes match my search criteria?

     d)   Students with a blue shape or a green shape hold it up to be counted. (Record the answer beside the search string.)

     e)   What happened to the results? (Answer: There are more.)

     f)   What did the OR do to the search? (Answer: OR broadened it.)

     g)   Why? (Answer: we were less specific or we allowed either one of two criteria to be met to make a match.)

6. Say to the students (and write the bolded search terms on the board):

     a)   I am searching for **round**. How many shapes match my search criteria? (Write the result on the board.)

     b)   I am searching for **round NOT small**. How many shapes match my search criteria?

     c)   Students with a large round shape hold it up to be counted. (Once again record the answer on the board beside that particular search string.)

     d)   What happened to the results? (Answer: There are fewer.)

     e)   What did the NOT do to the search? (Answer: NOT removed a specific subset from the group.)

7. Ask:

     a)   How do these terms apply when you are searching?

     b)   When would you use them?

Ask students to give examples or provide them yourself.

8. Go over the concepts of narrowing and broadening—get the students to explain them—give examples as appropriate (for example, school **NOT** secondary, UK **OR** United Kingdom, television **AND** violence).

ARE THERE ANY PITFALLS OR POINTERS?

- This activity is best used with Databases II: Simulated Searching (page 89)
- This activity may be used as an alternative to Boolean Frogs and Fish (page 97). It may be easier to use with a large group of students.
- Numbers of results that match the search criteria will differ depending on whether or not all shapes are handed out.

WHAT SAMPLES OR SUPPORT MATERIALS CAN I USE?

- Support Material 35: Boolean Attribute Shapes (see CD-ROM). Attribute shape sets should be made from colored cardboard and laminated to ensure long life. The support material should be duplicated on pink, blue, green, and yellow. There should be eight shapes in each color (four large, four small), thirty-two shapes in total.

16

Databases III

Now that your students know all about databases and how they function, here is their opportunity to practice using real live periodical databases from your library.

WHAT WILL THE STUDENTS LEARN?

Students will learn how to use a database and apply proper search techniques.

HOW MUCH TIME WILL I NEED?

You will need 60–90 minutes.

WHAT PREPARATION OR MATERIALS ARE REQUIRED?

- database worksheet
- computers—for instructor and for students
- LCD projector
- screen or white board to project onto

HOW DOES IT WORK?

1. Hand out worksheet and ask students to work through it, following the directions and answering the questions.
2. Stop the class at various points throughout the worksheet to explain or clarify details if necessary. (These details may have to do with the database itself, or more generally, with search technique or searching concepts.)
3. Have an answer key ready, either for going over the answers later with students or for students to check their own answers. If you have been stopping the students throughout the exercise to explain details, most problematic areas will already have been dealt with and the answer key should not provide the students with many surprises.

ARE THERE ANY PITFALLS OR POINTERS?

- The activity is best done after Databases I and II (see pages 77and 89).
- Please see the samples provided in the *What Samples or Support Materials Can I Use?* section (below). Naturally, each institution will have its own variety of databases and a unique student population; no support material can possibly be provided to meet all the needs that will arise in these different environments. Feel free to adapt these support materials as you see fit for your own particular circumstances.
- Both worksheets that follow were designed with the following aims in mind:
  - to explain the features of the database
  - to allow the students to discover these features by doing, not by reading explanations of them
  - to teach and review search techniques and concepts such as truncation, keyword versus field searching, narrowing or broadening a search, and so forth
  - to emphasize wherever possible training the students to read the search screen and rely on themselves to figure out how the various functions of the database work.

WHAT SAMPLES OR SUPPORT MATERIALS CAN I USE?

- Support Material 36: SIRS Discoverer Worksheet (sample; see CD-ROM)
- Support Material 37: SIRS Discoverer Worksheet—Answer Key (see CD-ROM)
- Support Material 38: Proquest 5000 Worksheets—Basic and Advanced (sample; see CD-ROM)
- Support Material 39: Proquest 5000 Worksheets—Basic and Advanced—Answer Key (see CD-ROM)

17

Search Strings

In order for your students to make the most of the information sources available to them, they will need to be effective searchers. Crucial to an effective search is an effective search string. Here's an activity that will start them in the right direction.

WHAT WILL THE STUDENTS LEARN?

- Students will identify concepts and vocabulary associated with searching electronic databases and the Internet.
- Students will create a variety of search strings.

HOW MUCH TIME WILL I NEED?

You will need 30 minutes.

WHAT PREPARATION OR MATERIALS ARE REQUIRED?

- four card sets:
  - Boolean Operators
  - Keywords
  - Related Terms
  - Truncation/wildcards
- Blu-Tak or similar adhesive putty
- white board
- white board markers
- white board eraser(s)

HOW DOES IT WORK?

1. Ask the students, "What is a search string?" (Answer: A statement that you use to search for information in a computerized database or on the Internet.)

2. Ask the students, "How do we come up with a search string?"

3. Write the following research topic on the board. (You will want to change the topic to one that is more appropriate for your region—if you do, Support Materials 41 to 43 will need to be changed accordingly.)
   The UAE should have a recycling program.

4. Ask the students to identify the keywords (write on board or stick up cards):
   UAE   recycling

5. Ask them to think about related words, synonyms, or broader and narrower terms. This can be done in either of two ways depending on the level of activity you want in the class:
   a) Students call out suggestions and words are listed on the board under each heading.
   OR
   b) Instructor says, "I've done the work for you. All you need to do is place your word under the correct keyword." (Give out cards to individual students and ask them to place the cards under the related keyword.)

   Results should look something like this:

UAE	*Recycling*
United Arab Emirates	environment
Gulf	waste disposal
Arabian peninsula	waste
Arab countries	plastics
Arabian gulf	glass
Middle East	paper
Dubai	green
	global warming
	pollution

6. Select a student to come up and develop a search string on the board.

7. While the student is engaged in this task, ask the class, "Do you need anything else apart from these words?" (Hopefully they will suggest Boolean operators such as AND/OR/NOT. Have a card for each of these words.)

8. Use student examples as much as possible to discuss:
   a) What happens to the search when we join two terms with AND?
   b) What about OR?
   c) What about NOT?

9. Use Boolean Attribute Shapes (page 103) or Boolean Frogs and Fish (page 97) to review the concept of Boolean logic if necessary.

10. Pause here and give out truncation cards. Ask students with the wildcards (*) to put them on the board in a row along the top. Tell the rest of the students to decide which wildcard their own keyword (that is, the card they have) should go under and to place it there. (Students will either recognize that there are word family associations between their word and the wildcard or they will remember what a wildcard is. If not, stop and review this concept.)

11. Ask the students to suggest and demonstrate how these wildcards could be incorporated into the existing search strings.

12. Discuss use of parentheses: When do you use parentheses? Give an example on the board:

environment AND (UAE OR united arab emirates)
(environment OR pollution) AND UAE

13. Invite the students to suggest another example of how to use parentheses for this search. Write their suggestion on the board.

14. Discuss use of quotation marks: When do you use quotation marks? (Answer: Use them around a group of words that you want to keep together as a phrase. Or, use them when you have two or more words that stand for only one idea and that must be kept together.) Give an example on the board:
    "waste disposal"
    "united arab emirates"

15. Ask the students to write down any others that they can think of.

Examples for instructor's reference:

Wildcard/Truncation

recycl* = recycle, recycling, recycled, recyclable
arab* = arabian, arab
environment* = environment, environmental, environmentally
plastic* = plastic, plastics
pollut* = pollute, pollution, polluting

Boolean phrases

uae OR united arab emirates
uae OR united arab emirates OR gulf OR middle east
uae AND recycling
gulf AND environment

Parentheses (i.e., brackets)

(uae OR united arab emirates) AND recycling
(uae OR united arab emirates OR gulf OR middle east) AND pollution

Quotation marks

A group of words:	**One idea:**
"united arab emirates"	= a country
"middle east"	= a region of the world
"waste disposal"	= a process
"global warming"	= a process

The following search strings might be useful for searching on this topic:
Write one or more on the board:

    (uae OR "united arab emirates") AND recycl*
    gulf AND (environment* OR recycl*)
    "global warming" AND recycl* AND (uae OR "united arab emirates")

ARE THERE ANY PITFALLS OR POINTERS?

- As mentioned, this example can and should be edited to make it relevant to instructor's circumstances (for example, geographical location, theme).

WHAT SAMPLES OR SUPPORT MATERIALS CAN I USE?

- Support Material 40: Card Set 1—Boolean Operators (duplicate this set ten times) (see CD-ROM)
- Support Material 41: Card Set 2—Keywords
- Support Material 42: Card Set 3—Related Terms
- Support Material 43: Card Set 4—Truncation/wildcards

SUPPORT MATERIAL 41:

SEARCH STRINGS—CARD SET 2—KEYWORDS

UAE

RECYCLING

SUPPORT MATERIAL 42:

SEARCH STRINGS—CARD SET 3—RELATED TERMS

Note: Support Materials 42 and 43 are included in their entirety in the attached CD-ROM (these pages show only a sampling).

environment

Arabian Gulf

SUPPORT MATERIAL 43:

SEARCH STRINGS—CARD SET 4—TRUNCATION/WILDCARDS

Note: Support Materials 42 and 43 are included in their entirety in the attached CD-ROM (these pages show only a sampling).

recycl*

Arab*

18

Advanced Searching

Here's an excellent self-paced activity that will help students review and refine their understanding of searching in electronic resources.

WHAT WILL THE STUDENTS LEARN?

- Students will gain practice predicting potential problems that could arise during a search and identifying possible solutions to these problems.
- Students will gain practice evaluating the potential usefulness of search results by looking critically at the citation information, in particular the title and source.

HOW MUCH TIME WILL I NEED?

You will need 30 minutes.

WHAT PREPARATION OR MATERIALS ARE REQUIRED?

- Advanced Searching card set
- answer key

HOW DOES IT WORK?

1. Hand out card sets (Support Material 44)—one to each group of two or three students.
2. Explain that each card contains a research question and a suggested search string or search terms used by the searcher.
3. Explain that the students must follow the instructions, first of all thinking about potential problems with the search, then going on to look at search results and to evaluate their potential usefulness based on the information in the results list. (This works best if the students are directed to look at card 1A, then go on to 1B, rather than view the whole card at once. This means the instructor must cut the cards into

two parts. See the first point in the *What Samples or Support Materials Can I Use?* section, below.)

4. Ask the students to list suggestions for ways to repeat the search, avoiding irrelevant results and finding more useful ones.

5. Tell the students that on completion of one research question (for example, 1A/1B) they may correct their work using the answer key and repeat the exercise using a different research question (for example, 2A/2B).

ARE THERE ANY PITFALLS OR POINTERS?

- After initial explanation this activity may be done independently and students may use the answer keys to correct their work.
- Alternatively, the instructor may wish to direct the activity and discuss the results with the group.
- Please note that a generic form has been provided for instructors who wish to use their own search examples. The examples provided below are not actual searches but have been constructed to imitate the kinds of problems one could encounter.
- A suggested add-on to this activity is to have the students do the searches they suggest (in the latter part of each B card) in one of the library's databases to see if the problems that were anticipated can be avoided using their approach. If so, the instructor may prefer to use real search examples from the library databases for the card sets, rather than the artificially constructed ones below.

WHAT SAMPLES OR SUPPORT MATERIALS CAN I USE?

- Support Material 44: Card Set—Advanced Searching (each set consists of three research questions and sample searches)
  - Photocopy and laminate the card sets. Two to three students is the maximum for each card set; therefore, the number required of each set will depend on how many students there are.
  - This activity works best if the instructor cuts each card into two parts (along the bold line one-third of the way down the card)—for example, 1A and 1B, 2A and 2B. Students should be instructed to look at the 1A card first, followed by the 1B card, and work through the cards in this manner.
- Support Material 45: Advanced Searching Answer Key (see CD-ROM)
  - You may wish to photocopy several copies of this—one for each group of students. The answer key does not have to be cut up.

SUPPORT MATERIAL 44:
ADVANCED SEARCHING

Note: The following is a sampling only; see the rest of Support Material 44 on the accompanying CD-ROM.

Research question:

How do spiders build their webs and what do they use them for?

| 1A |

Search string used by searcher:

spider AND web

Can you think of any problems you might encounter with this search? What kind of articles do you think these terms might find in the database?

_____

_____

_____

Search results:

1. *The post-spider world*; Nate Zelnick; **Internet World** Dec. 1, 2000; Vol. 6, Iss. 23; pg. 72
2. *Webcaster*; Jeff Jensen; **Entertainment Weekly** Nov. 24, 2000; Iss. 570; pg. 85
3. *Wasps turn spiders into slaves*; Anonymous; **Current Science**, Middletown; Jan. 5, 2001; Vol. 86, Iss. 9; pg. 13

Evaluate each of the above citations. Are they all useful? If not, why? (Hint: Look at the titles and the sources.)

1. _____

2. _____

3. _____

Possible solutions:

How can you make this search better so that you avoid the irrelevant articles and find more useful ones? Write the search terms and strings you would use below:

_____

_____

_____

| 1B |

19

Types of Information and Where To Find Them
(Beyond the Library Shelves)

This activity is good for exploring the differences among the Internet, primary sources, and databases in terms of reliability, currency, and scope of content. Also, it helps students to understand that there are often several places the same information can be found.

WHAT WILL THE STUDENTS LEARN?

- Students will be able to identify the most appropriate sources for a variety of types of information that can be accessed beyond the library shelves.
- Students will become aware of the need to treat all information critically, especially that found on the Internet.

HOW MUCH TIME WILL I NEED?

You will need 15 to 30 minutes.

WHAT PREPARATION OR MATERIALS ARE REQUIRED?

- card sets
  - Information sources
  - Information need/Types of information
- Blu-Tak or similar adhesive type putty
- white board

HOW DOES IT WORK?

1. Stick the three cards showing the different sources of information on the board (Internet, Periodical Database, Primary Sources).
2. Ask the students:
   a) What is the Internet?
   b) What is a periodical database? (Here we are referring to the online databases that we access through the library Web site.)
   c) What is a primary source?
3. Brainstorm on the board: What kind of information could you find in each category? (Make the list very brief.)
4. Hand out cards containing all the different information needs and types of information (use as many or as few as you like). Explain that the students must decide on the best place to find the particular information needs or types of information that they have been given.
5. Give the class a few minutes to discuss among themselves. They must come to the board and stick their type of information under the most appropriate source (that is, Internet, Periodical Database, or Primary Source).

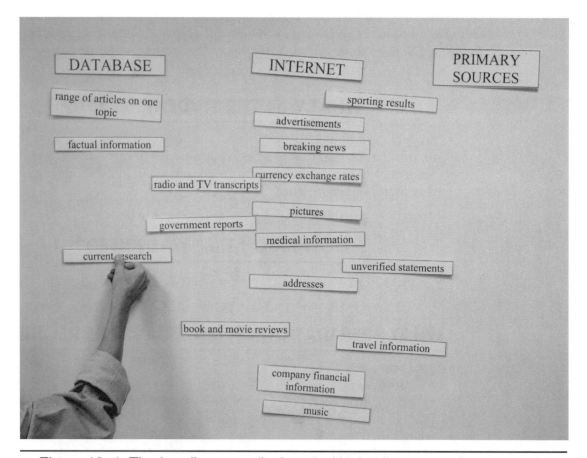

Figure 19–1. The headings are displayed with details arranged underneath.

(Note: This may be a difficult decision and some students may end up choosing to place their card between two sources. This is all right. Some cards could conceivably be put under all three headings.)

6. Discuss where each type of information has been put. Should any be moved? As each one is discussed it will become clear that most types of information can be found in most of these places.

7. Select some specific examples and ask where would be the best place to find each type and why? For example:
    a) **breaking news** (Answer: The Internet because of immediacy/constant updating/ ability for live action, and so forth.)
    b) **medical information** (Answer: Primary source—consult the doctor yourself.)
    c) **factual information, research** (Answer: Periodical database as opposed to the Internet because there has already been a certain level of verification done before information can get included in the database. If you rely on the Internet you may or may not have accurate and reliable information.)

8. Discuss:
    a) Differences between the Internet and databases, such as who can publish a Web page? (Answer: Anyone.) Anyone could write a page on the best diet for diabetes, but the information might not be correct because that author may not know much about the subject and may not have medical qualifications. There is a great deal of excellent information available over the Web but **students need to be very critical of everything found on the Internet.**
    b. Who makes up a database? (Answer: A company, an organization.) Who decides what information goes into the database? (Answer: The editor or compiler.) Do they seek expert opinion? (Answer: Yes.) Does this mean everything in a database is accurate or true? (Answer: No.) Students must always be critical of any information they read or are told, but there is more control over what goes into a database, making it more likely to be authoritative, accurate, and reliable.

ARE THERE ANY PITFALLS OR POINTERS?

- You may wish to use different headings (such as, sources) depending on the students' level of understanding of these terms.

WHAT SAMPLES OR SUPPORT MATERIALS CAN I USE?

- Support Material 46: Information Sources—Headings Cards (colored paper)
- Support Material 47: Information Need/Types of Information (black and white)

SUPPORT MATERIAL 46:

TYPES OF INFORMATION AND WHERE TO FIND THEM—INFORMATION SOURCES—HEADINGS CARDS (COLORED PAPER)

Note: This material has been reduced in size; see the accompanying CD-ROM for the full-sized version.

PERIODICAL DATABASE

PRIMARY SOURCES

INTERNET

SUPPORT MATERIAL 47:
TYPES OF INFORMATION AND WHERE TO FIND THEM—INFORMATION NEED/TYPES OF INFORMATION (BLACK AND WHITE)

Note: This is a sampling only; the full material can be found on the accompanying CD-ROM.

book and movie reviews

medical information

weather reports

sporting results

travel information

20

Bibliography and Citation

Here is another experiential activity that helps students discover the purposes of a bibliography or reference list and the parts that are essential to a citation.

WHAT WILL THE STUDENTS LEARN?

- Students will identify a number of reasons for creating a bibliography as part of their research process.
- Students will identify fields of information that enable a reader to trace a specific source.

HOW MUCH TIME WILL I NEED?

You will need 40 to 60 minutes.

WHAT MATERIALS OR PREPARATION ARE REQUIRED?

- Reasons for a Bibliography card set
- Blu-Tak or similar adhesive putty
- citation puzzles
- white board
- library's periodical collection

HOW DOES IT WORK?

1. Hand a card (from card set Reasons for a Bibliography—Support Material 49) to the students as they enter the classroom.
2. Ask the students, "What is a bibliography?"

3. Explain that the cards they hold give reasons why it is important to create a bibliography when doing research. But some of these cards are "red herrings."

4. Ask the students to look carefully at their card and decide if it is a good reason for writing a bibliography or not.

5. Put the two headings on the board: **Bibliographies are usually used for** and **Bibliographies are not usually used for**.

6. Invite the students to come to the front and fix their cards to the board under the correct heading.

7. Discuss the choices and move any cards that the class decides are incorrectly placed.

8. Elicit that the common factor among all the reasons for having a bibliography is the ability to find a source.

9. Now tell the students that you want them to work in groups of three or four (depending on the size of the class) to find a source.

10. Hand out pieces of the citation puzzle (Support Material 50) to each group. (Using a different color for each citation puzzle oval makes this activity easier.) Withhold the pieces containing the date and page information.

11. Explain that you have given the students some pieces of a puzzle and by putting the pieces together they should be able to find a particular source of information (in this case, a journal article). Ask them what sort of information they have on each piece. (Answer: Title of article, author, and source.)

12. Review the procedure for locating periodicals according to your particular library (for example, ours are shelved in a separate collection, alphabetically by title).

13. Ask the students to go in their groups to the library's periodicals and find the journal article on their puzzle pieces. Stress to students that if they find they need **extra pieces** of information in order to trace the article, they should ask the instructor and the instructor will provide them. (Don't tell them that you have the date and page number for each article, but give them these pieces if they ask.)

14. Move through the groups as they are working and ask them how they are progressing. (There should be high levels of frustration as they struggle to identify a specific article from a huge bundle of back issues of the particular journal title.) Again, ask if there is any piece of information that might make their job easier.

15. When someone requests the date, volume, and so forth, ask all groups if they would also like that information and hand out those puzzle pieces. Some groups may find the article at this stage but others may need the page number as well. If frustration levels get too high, ask if a page number would help.

16. Return to the classroom to discuss the results. (Some students may enjoy or insist on putting all the pieces of their puzzle together to complete the oval shape.)

17. Summarize the information that is needed in a bibliographic citation to enable the reader to trace the source of information. (Mention at this point that different types of sources require different details but the purpose is the same.)

ARE THERE ANY PITFALLS OR POINTERS?

- The reasons for a bibliography may be expanded depending on the size of the group because there are many ways to restate these general concepts.

- Similarly, and especially if the students are second-language speakers of English, you may wish to omit some of the Reasons for a Bibliography cards since many are duplications of the same concept, simply worded differently. Choose the simplest to get the point across for ESL students.
- The citation puzzles must be created using the support material provided and applying details of journal articles held in your own library collection.
- This activity will be more successful if the articles selected are from journals that the library has been subscribing to for some time (that is, journals for which the library has substantial back files).

WHAT SAMPLES OR SUPPORT MATERIAL CAN I USE?

- Support Material 48: Headings Cards—Bibliographies are/are not usually used for . . . (see CD-ROM)
- Support Material 49: Reasons for a Bibliography Cards (see CD-ROM)
- Support Material 50: Generic Oval Citation Puzzle
  To make your own puzzle pieces:
  - Type the relevant information for each journal article into the oval as per the support material provided on the CD-ROM
  - You will have a different oval for each journal article
  - Copy each oval onto a different color of paper
  - Laminate and cut.

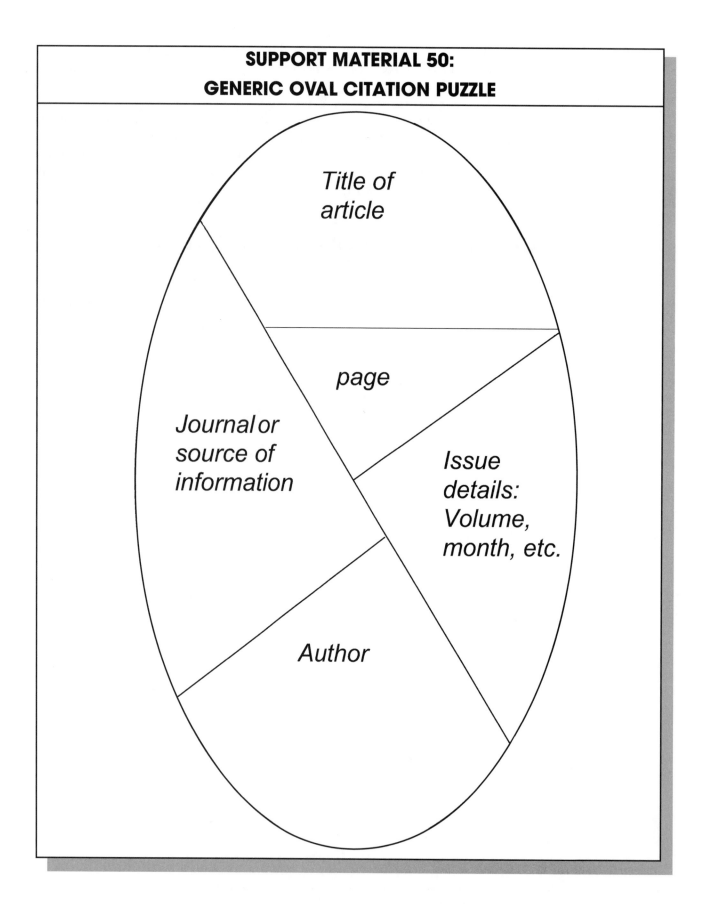

References and Further Reading

American Library Association. Presidential Committee on Information Literacy. 1989. *Final Report.* Chicago: The American Library Association. Available: www.ala.org/acrl/nili/ilit1st.html [20 November 2001].

Bostonian, R., et al. 2000. *Association of College and Research Libraries: Standards for College Libraries 2000 Edition.* Chicago: Association of College and Research Libraries. Available: www.ala.org/acrl/guides/college.html [2 September 2000].

Breivik, P. 1998. *Student Learning in the Information Age.* Phoenix, Ariz.: The Oryx Press.

Carey, J. 1998. "Library Skills, Information Skills, and Information Literacy: Implications for Teaching and Learning." *School Library Media Quarterly (Online).* Available: www.ala.org/aasl/SLMQ/skills.html [6 May 2000].

Carr, Jo Ann. 1998. "Information Literacy and Teacher Education." *ERIC Digest* ED 97–4. Washington, D.C.: ERIC Clearinghouse on Teaching and Teacher Education.

Gradowski, G., L. Snavely, and P. Dempsey, eds. 1998. *Designs for Active Learning: A Sourcebook of Classroom Strategies for Information Education.* Chicago: Association of College and Research Libraries.

Henri, J. and K. Bonanno, eds. 1999. *The Information Literate School Community: Best Practice.* Wagga Wagga, Australia: Center for Information Studies.

Iannuzzi, P., C. Mangrum, and S. Strichart. 1999. *Teaching Information Literacy Skills.* Boston: Allyn and Bacon.

Iannuzzi, P., S. Strichart, and C. Mangrum. 1998. *Teaching Study Skills and Strategies in College.* Boston: Allyn and Bacon.

Information Literacy at Florida International University. July 16,1999. Florida International University Libraries. Available: www.fiu.edu/~library/ili/iliprop.html [21 February 2000].

Information Literacy on the WWW. February 6, 2000. Florida International University Libraries. Available: www.fiu.edu/~library/ili/iliweb.html [24 February 2000].

Institute for Information Literacy. August 3, 2000. Chicago: Association of College and Research Libraries. Available: www.ala.org/acrl/nili/nilihp.html [11 May 2000].

Libutti, P. and B. Gratch, eds. 1995. *Teaching Information Retrieval and Evaluation Skills to Education Students and Practitioners: A Casebook of Applications.* Chicago: American Library Association.

Mangrum, C., P. Iannuzzi, and S. Strichart. 1998. *Teaching Study Skills and Strategies in Grades 4–8.* Boston: Allyn and Bacon.

Phillips, Gary. 1984. *Growing Hope.* Minneapolis, Minn.: National Youth Leadership Council.

Pritchett, P. 1993. *Culture Shift.* Dallas: Pritchett and Associates.

Royce, John. 1999. "Reading As a Basis for Using Information Technology Efficiently." In *The Information Literate School Community: Best Practice,* edited by J. Henri and K. Bonanno. Wagga Wagga, Australia: Center for Information Studies.

Siegfried, John J., Phillip Saunders, Ethan Stinar, and Hao Zhang. 1996. "Teaching Tools: How Is Introductory Economics Taught in America?" *Economic Enquiry* 43: 182–192.

Strichart S. S., C. Mangrum, and P. Iannuzzi. 1997. *Teaching Study Skills and Strategies in High School*. Boston: Allyn and Bacon.

Warmkessel, M. M. and J. M. McCade. 1997. "Integrating Information Literacy into the Curriculum." *Research Strategies*, 15, no. 2: 80–88.

Young, Rosemary M. and Stephena Harmony. 1999. *Working with Faculty to Design Undergraduate Information Literacy Programs*. New York: Neal-Schuman.

Index

About the Authors

JANE BIRKS has ten years' experience as a teacher-librarian in an elementary school in Australia. She was also a co-director and teacher in a computer education / Internet service provision business.

FIONA HUNT has taught information literacy for six years prior to her current employment as an academic librarian.

Jane and Fiona are presently information literacy librarians at Zayed University in the United Arab Emirates, creating and developing information literacy programs. They were invited to participate in the ACRL "Invitational Best Practice" at the ALA Annual, June 2002. They will present "Information Literacy: International Perspectives" at the 2003 ALA/CLA Annual Conference in Toronto.

025.524
B6193

105433

LINCOLN CHRISTIAN COLLEGE AND SEMINARY

3 4711 00165 2009